A PRUDENT REBEL

THE SECRET & SUBVERSIVE WRITINGS OF FONTENELLE

BERNARD LE BOVIER DE FONTENELLE

(1657-1757)

TRANSLATED BY

KIRK WATSON

2019

Contents

TRANSLATOR'S INTRODUCTION

Bernard Le Bouyer de Fontenelle (1657-1757), although now an obscure figure, was once considered "one of the greatest philosophers on earth" (Vauvenargues)[1], "the most universal mind of the century" (Voltaire)[2] "a sage worthy to serve as a model for philosophers"[3], for example. With Pierre and Thomas Corneille as his uncles, he originally hoped for success as an author for the stage, but after a notorious failure there, he focused on other forms of writing. His fame finally came as a popularizer of science, as the writer who most successfully synthesized the humanities and science, style and learning, especially in his *Conversations on the Plurality of Worlds* (1686) and many *éloges* in favor of contemporary scientists and thinkers.

He was accepted into the French Academy in 1691, becoming its "perpetual secretary" for forty years.

---

[1] Gilbert Luc de Clapiers Vauvenargues, *Oeuvres de Vauvenargues* (1857), p. 276
https://books.google.com/books?id=Tde5jbTgNC8Candpg=PA276

[2] *Catalogue de la plupart des écrivains Français qui ont paru dans le siècle de Louis XIV...* in *Œuvres complètes de Voltaire avec des remarques et des notes historiques, scientifiques et littéraires: Siècle de Louis XIV* (1826), p. 131.

[3] Sylvain Maréchal, "Fontenelle", *Dictionnaire des athées anciens et modernes* (1800), p.149.

However, as Sainte-Beuve once said, "there are two completely distinct Fontenelles": despite his success and prominence, his elevated social position, and his lifelong profession of Catholic orthodoxy[4], Fontenelle secretly wrote and distributed a body of influential, subversive texts, attacking superstition, Christianity, political institutions, and conventional morality.

In a certain an old French Dictionary[5], the entry for "the Prudent" describes "a peaceful and secret association of freethinkers, who hide under their mantles the torch of the truth, for fear it be extinguished amid the storms of politics", and that this "numerous" sect was perhaps best represented by Fontenelle. It's been written that he fought this intellectual battle "without making any great noise about it"[6]; indeed, he was quoted as having said that "if his hand were full of truths, he would be very careful to keep it closed"[7].

This was prudence rather than cowardice; several of his known writings had already placed a target on his back; Voltaire writes that in 1713, Fontenelle "was on the point of losing his pensions, his position and his liberty, for having written...twenty years earlier, the *Treatise on*

---

[4] An account of his death records his dying wish: "I therefore declare to you that I have lived & wish to die in the faith of the Catholic, Apostolic & Roman Church." (From Louis Moréri's *Grand dictionnaire historique*, Vol. 5, "Fontenelle", p. 236; online: http://artflsrv02.uchicago.edu/cgi-bin/extras/moreripag.pl?TOME_05_Page_0236.jpg)

[5] Sylvain Maréchal, ibid., "Prudens", p. 371.

[6] Jonathan Israel, *Radical Enlightenment*, p. 167.

[7] *Œuvres de Fontenelle*, Volume 1 (Salmon, 1829), p. xxxviii.

Oracles... A Jesuit had written against Fontenelle, he hadn't deigned to reply; and this was enough for the...confessor of Louis XIV, to accuse Fontenelle of atheism to the king"[8]. His famous amicable good-naturedness apparently preserved him; he survived this episode only because of a friendly intervention by the Lieutenant of the Police[9].

In the above-mentioned book on oracles, he had dared to argue that the ancient pagan oracles had naturalistic explanations, not demonic ones. In addition to that notorious book, he secretly wrote and distributed satires, speeches, letters, treatises, even a utopian novel, all of which ruthlessly attacked the society, morals, and religion of his contemporaries and his country.

The first text presented here, "On the Existence of God", sets the outer boundaries of Fontenelle's radicalism: he rejects the materialistic, naturalistic ideas of the spontaneous generation of life and the origin of the world through the chance concurrence of matter. He claims that biological science demonstrates the need for a creator God.

The second text, "A Letter to the Marquis de la Fare on the Resurrection" is a light-hearted letter he wrote to a friend, offering various speculations about the doctrine of

---

[8] Voltaire, *Dictionnaire philosophique*, "Philosophes"
[9] Voltaire, *Letters addressed to the Prince of ***, containing comments on the writings of the most eminent authors who have been accused of attacking the Christian religion* (1767), 8th letter, on Fontenelle.

the resurrection. It treats, among other things, the question of where everyone would fit on earth if they were all to reappear bodily at the same time.

The third text, "On the Origin of the Fables", is harshly dismissive of pagan myth, arguing they contain no hidden wisdom, but only the "chimeras, reveries and absurdities" produced in the idiotic childhood of humanity. People only see miracles "in proportion to [their] ignorance and lack of experience", therefore they gradually fall away as a nation becomes wiser and better informed. Gods simply reflect the values of their worshipers. Fontenelle notes that the invention of writing halted the development of mythology, crystallized it as it then was, and led to rational type of history and a taste for factual accuracy.

Next, "On the diversity of Religions" was a prize-winning speech delivered by and published under the name of Fontenelle's friend, Jacques Brunel. Its subversive irony went unnoticed at the time, but it was appreciated later by abbé Raynal, in his *Nouvelles littéraires*, as "One of the boldest and most philosophical pieces ever written in this country"[10], who, along with modern scholarship, attributes it to Fontenelle.

---

[10] In *Correspondance littéraire, Philosophique et critique*, 27 Juillet 1750. Online at:
https://books.google.com/books?id=cuEwUAN7pF0Candpg=RA1-PA51; see also Alain Mothu, Alain Sandrier. *Minora clandestina: le philosophe antichrétien et autres écrits iconoclastes de l'âge classique* (Champion, 2003), p. 80.

"An Account of the Island of Borneo", similarly treats the problem with religious diversity. It expresses, as one modern writer puts it "through allegorical fiction, a fundamental anticlericalism and hostility to the religious spirit, only hinted at in his earlier writings"[11]. In this brief tale, the tyrannical queen Mreo (an anagram for "Rome") fights a late-coming rival Eenegue ("Geneva") over the succession from her ancestor Mliseo (a kind of anagram for "Jerusalem", i.e. Judaism). Fontenelle sent this text as a face-value history of Borneo to Pierre Bayle for publication; the latter innocently published it in his *Nouvelles de la République des Lettres*. This text was cited along with the book on oracles, in the above-mentioned attempt to punish Fontenelle decades later.

In the next selection, "A Treatise on Liberty", Fontenelle argues for materialistic and deterministic positions, openly combating the idea of free will, arguing that mental dispositions govern all we do, and that morality is dubious at best. It is said to have been published originally in 1700 and immediately withdrawn, shredded, and burned on the order of the Parisian *Parlement*. It was later published in the influential and scandalous free-thinking collection *Nouvelles Libertés de Penser* in 1743[12]. Fontenelle was only detected as its author long afterwards.

---

[11] Kors, Alan Charles. *Encyclopedia of the Enlightenment.* OUP (2003), "Fontenelle", p. 54.
[12] Available in English in my *New Liberties in Thought* https://www.amazon.com/dp/B07397HK7K.

Next, "On Happiness", is a gem in Fontenelle's *œuvre*, offering a moderately hedonistic moral code. Happiness is described as a more or less permanent state, from which most people are necessarily excluded. Happiness is largely independent of us, but philosophy can help a certain number of lucky people. Others have to make do as they can with fleeting and rejuvenating moments of pleasure. Philosophical techniques for happiness are discussed, such as minimizing suffering by eliminating all imaginary evils, by foreseeing and mitigating all possible real pains, and focusing on the good we can truly expect. It's all a question of calculation, of wisdom. The best way to find lasting contentment is to take pleasure in the readily available, simple pleasures of life.

The next selection is an award-winning speech entitled "On Patience". Fontenelle attacks the Stoic kind of patience and constancy as chimerical, and, at least on a surface reading, he presents Christian patience, with its love of pain, as superior. Some have read this text as both a ploy to gain entry into the French Academy, and even an ironic exposition of Christian morality[13].

The next and longest text, the centerpiece of this collection, is a long-forgotten utopian novel[14]. *The Story*

---

[13] See *Fontenelle: Textes choisis et commentés par Émile Faguet* (1912), p. 173.
https://babel.hathitrust.org/cgi/pt?id=mdp.39015030369238and view=1upandseq=185

[14] Which was probably influenced by a famous contemporary utopian novel, Denis Vairasse's *History of the Sevarambians* (1675).

of the Ajaoians tells of a Dutch explorer who shipwrecks on an unknown island and is welcomed by the natives. The bulk of the book is a description of the religion, customs, and government of this people, who are atheists[15] or perhaps pantheists, revering Nature only.

Pierre Bayle had suggested in his 1682 book, *A Letter on the Comet,* that, since all humans regardless of religion or belief are most deeply motivated by worldly drives such as love of praise or reward, fear of shame or punishment, therefore, provided it had strict and properly enforced laws, there is no reason why a society of atheists wouldn't work as well as any other. Thus, the "Story of the Ajaoians", thought to have been written the following year, can be read as a fictional portrayal of this idea of a religionless society, indeed, a society based explicitly on materialism and pantheism.

The Story of the Ajaoians was published posthumously in 1768, nearly a century after it was written. While, as it was "unpublished and unknown," having made "no known impact during the Early Enlightenment"[16], it remains an interesting specimen in the history of ideas. This was "philosophically, the most audacious of the

---

[15] The name of the island and people, Ajao, is thought to have been constructed by the author from the word Jao, i.e. Jehovah, with the privative A-, as in atheist. See Hans-Günter Fünke, «Un manuscrit retrouvé: "L'Histoire des Ajaoiens" de Fontenelle, utopie d'une republique d'athées vertueux», in *La philosophie clandestine à l'Age classique : actes du colloque de l'Université Jean Monnet Saint-Etienne du 29 septembre au 2 octobre 1993.*
[16] Israel, ibid., p. 593.

French Spinozist novels of the Early Enlightenment", a reflection of "the early and forceful emergence of radical ideas in France during the 1680s"[17].

The island of Ajao functions on a communistic model, with multiple families sharing large houses, the State housing and educating the youth, and everyone contributing to and taking from the common stock. It is an ambiguous utopia; the Ajaoian women are truly second to men in these utopian institutions, and the book relates how the island's aborigines were despoiled and enslaved by the Ajaoians; although their living conditions were softened, the natives remain enslaved and controlled amid this paradise.

The final text, "A Fragment of what Fontenelle called his Republic", outlines a sort of utopia, somewhat similar to the Ajaoians' government in its communism and simple hierarchies, which is thought by some to be a precursor to the work on the Ajaoians.

Fontenelle was a worthy herald of the Enlightenment; in his old age he was openly recognized as such by the younger generation. The moralist Vauvenargues said that "Fontenelle deserves to be regarded by posterity as one of the greatest philosophers on earth… to him we owe, in large part, this philosophical spirit leading to contempt for declamations and authorities, to dispute truth with precision"[18]. In a eulogy, Friedrich Grimm wrote

---

[17] Ibid., pp. 591ff.
[18] Gilbert Luc de Clapiers Vauvenargues, *Oeuvres de*

that: "people, once so ignorant and limited...have taken from his works the principles of a sound and enlightened philosophy. The philosophical spirit, now so widespread, thus owes its first steps to Mr. de Fontenelle"[19].

Vauvenargues (Furne, 1857), p. 276
[19] Friedrich Melchior Freiherr von Grimm, *Correspondance littéraire, philosophique et critique*, Feb. 1757.

ON THE EXISTENCE OF GOD

(1690s[20])

Metaphysics provides very solid proofs for the existence of God; but since this science is necessarily quite subtle and based on rather refined ideas, it looks suspicious to most Men, who believe that whatever isn't sensible and tangible must be chimerical and purely imaginary. I've seen many go to such extremes on this point in their metaphysical proofs, but who were in no way convinced, since they had always thought they were being fooled by hidden subtleties. There is reason to hope that such characters will find to their taste an argument from physics that is very clear, very intelligible, and based on ideas that are very familiar to everyone; one might also boast of its solidity and force, if it wasn't thought to have been invented.

Animals reproduce only by means of generation; but the first pair of each species must necessarily have been produced, either by the fortuitous concourse of the parts

---

[20] Per Trublet's *Memoires* in Moréri's *Grand dictionnaire*. Online at: http://artflsrv02.uchicago.edu/cgi-bin/extras/moreripag.pl?TOME_05_Page_0234.jpg

of matter, or by the will of an intelligent Being who disposes matter according to his plans.

If the fortuitous concourse of the parts of matter produced the first animals, then why it doesn't produce more of them? And this isn't the only basis of my argument. It would be easy to reply that when the Earth was formed, it was then full of lively and active atoms, impregnated with the same subtle matter of which the Stars had just been made; in a word, while it was young and vigorous, it might have been fertile enough to push, out beyond itself, the various species of animals; and that after this first production, which depended on so many lucky and unique concourses, its fecundity might have been lost and exhausted; that, for example, we see certain newly dried marshes, the productive force of which is very different then from how it will be after fifty years of farming.

But I assert that when the Earth, as is supposed, produced the animals, it must have been in the same state as it now enjoys. It is certain that the Earth could only have produced the animals when it was in a position to nourish them; or at least it is certain that those who were the first stem of the species were only produced by the Earth at a time when they might also have been nourished by it. And, for the Earth to nourish the animals, it must provide them with many different plants, it must supply them with fresh water to drink; the air must also have a certain degree of fluidity, warmth, and weight, to be equally suitable for all these animals, the life of which is well known to be connected to all these qualities.

From the moment the Earth is assumed to be covered with all the plants necessary for animal subsistence, watered by the springs and rivers apt to quench their thirst, surrounded by an air they could breathe, it is therefore in the same state as we now see it; for these three things alone entail an infinity of others with which they have relationships and intertwinings. A single straw cannot grow if it isn't in concert, so to speak, with the rest of nature. There must be certain saps in the ground, a certain movement in these saps, neither too strong nor too slow, a certain Sun to imprint this movement, a certain medium by which the Sun acts. See how many relationships are involved, even though they go unnoticed. The air couldn't have the qualities by which it contributes to the life of animals unless it had in itself the same mixture of both subtle matter and thick vapors, and that which causes its weight, a quality that is as necessary as any other for the animals, and necessary in a certain degree, hadn't had the same action. It is clear that all of this would lead us even further from equality to equality; especially the springs and rivers which the animals couldn't have done without, which certainly originated nowhere other than in rain, the animals could only have been born after rain had fallen, that is, a considerable time after the formation of the Earth, consequently, when it was in a condition of consistency, and when this chaos, in favor of which the animals would be made from nothing, has ended completely.

It is true that newly dried marshes produce more than they will at a later period; but they are always somewhat productive, and it would be enough for the Earth to do the same: besides, the greater fecundity of freshly dried marshes is due to the quantity of salts they had amassed from rain, or the movement of the air, and which they had preserved unused. But the Earth has always the same quantity of corpuscles or atoms needed to form the animals; and its fertility, far from being lost, must in no way be diminished. What is an animal made of? An infinity of corpuscles which were distributed in the plants it ate, in the waters it drank, in the air it breathed; it's a composite parts of which have come from a thousand different places in our world. These atoms circulate constantly, they form, now a plant, now an animal, and having once formed the one, they are no less apt to form the other. Therefore, it isn't atoms of a particular nature that produce animals; it's only indifferent matter, of which all things are made successively, and the quantity of which is very clearly undiminished, since it always provides everywhere for everything equally. The atoms, the concurrence of which is supposed to have produced, at the beginning of the world, the first animals, are contained in this same matter which produces all the generations in our world; since when these first animals died, the machines of their bodies were disassembled and resolved into particles which were dispersed into the earth, the water, and the air. Thus, we still have these precious atoms, from which so many amazing machines would be formed; we have them in the same quantity, as suitable as ever to form these machines; they still form them every day by means of nourishment: all things are in the same state as when they came to be formed by a fortuitous concurrence. Why then should they not still be formed from time to time from similar concurrences?

It might be objected that some animals are born by means different from generation; scoters, worms which are produced on meat, in fruit, etc. But the force of my argument doesn't require that all animals of all species must be born by the route of generation; it's sufficient if even one species is perpetuated by this means only, and which consequently couldn't have been produced by the blind motion of matter. We are on a far surer footing, and certainly a great number of known species are only perpetuated by generation, and our proof is strengthened all the more.

But there is more; all the animals which seem to emerge, either from decay, or from humid and heated dust, come only from seeds that weren't perceived.

It has been discovered that the scoters lay eggs which this species of bird produces in the desert islands of the far north: and worms never appear in meat where flies haven't been able to leave their eggs. It's the same with all other animals that are thought to be born outside the way of generation. All modern experiments conspire to disabuse us of this ancient error, and I am sure that soon the least doubt will not remain on this subject.

But if any should remain, if there were animals coming outside the means of generation, the argument I've given would only be stronger. Either these animals are only ever born by this means of fortuitous concurrences, or they are born both this means and by that of generation. If they are always born from fortuitous concurrences, why would we now find in matter a disposition which does not produce them in the same way as it did at the beginning of the world? And why, when it comes to all the other animals that are supposed to have been born in this way, are all the dispositions of matter so altered that they are always born in a different way now? If they are born both by this way of fortuitous concurrences, and that of generation, why haven't all the other species of animals retained this double means of birth? Why is the more natural one, the only one that's consistent with the first origin of the animals, now lost for nearly all species?

I've given great extent to this proof and by so doing I will have caused offense in the minds of some who believe that the quantity of words is a sign of the weakness of arguments; but I beg them to consider that this argument is only lengthy because of the quibbles it has to prevent, and not the difficulty of the things being established.

I have not sought, fearing to interrupt the thread, to introduce a thought which strengthens it a great deal, prefering to share it now, separately. It wouldn't have sufficed for the Earth not to have produced the animals until it was in a certain disposition it no longer enjoys; thus, it should also produce them in a state when they could have fed on what it offered them: it should, for example, have produced the first man only at the age of one or two, where he could have satisfied, although with difficulty, his needs, and kept himself alive. Given the weakness which newborn children inherit, it would be worthless to set it in the middle of a meadow covered in lush plants, beside the best waters on earth, it certainly wouldn't live very long: for, our supposition excludes the she-wolf of Romulus and Remus, even she probably couldn't have saved herself from death that would have awaited her at her own birth. But how could the laws of motion initially produce a child of the age of one or two? How would they produce it even in the state it's presently in when it comes into the world? They plainly only lead things along by degrees, and there are no productions of nature which, from the weakest and most remote beginnings, aren't led slowly through an infinity of changes, all of which are inevitable, until their final perfection. If man were formed by the blind concourse of various parts of matter, then he would have to have begun by this atom, where life is only remarked in the nearly imperceptible motion of a single point; and I don't think anyone's imagination is so false as to conceive from where this living atom, cast at random upon the Earth, might have found blood or chyle, the only food suited to it, ready-made, or how it might have been able to grow, exposed as it would have been to all the injuries from the atmosphere. Here is a difficulty that will only get harder and harder; the more profoundly it is studied, the more it will require the intervention of a capable physicist. The fortuitous concourse of atoms cannot, therefore, have produced the animals; these works must have come from the hand of an intelligent Being, that is, God himself. The heavens and the Stars are more dazzling objects for the eyes; but they might lack the surest indices for the reason of the action of their author. The greatest works are not always the ones that say the most about their maker. If I see a mountain flattened, I don't know if that happened by the order of some prince, or due to an earthquake; but I can be sure that a prince ordered it when I see a small column bearing two lines of inscribed writing. It seems to me that the animals bear, so to speak, the clearest inscription, and which best teach us that there is a God, Author of the Universe.

A LETTER FROM FONTENELLE TO THE MARQUIS DE LA FARE ON THE RESURRECTION.

(~1705-10)[21]

You, who have a better imagination than anyone, you also doubt more intelligently than others. I am charmed by your difficulty about the immense space that would one day be necessary to contain all these men together, who, having only existed successively, from the creation, haven't failed to occupy a large part of the universe. Given your own size, how could you not be worried about this compression? If everyone had your volume, I'm also worried that my elbows couldn't swing freely: while waiting, I've thought that it would be good to have my own problem with it; here's mine.

When it pleases the Supreme Being to return to each spirit the body it formerly animated, how should he approach the job? Our bodies are composed today of

---

[21] Alain Mothu, "Badinages Sacrilèges sur la résurrection des corps", in *L'identification du texte clandestin aux XVIIe et XVIIIe siècles: Actes de la journée de Créteil du 15 mai 1998* (Presses Paris Sorbonne, 1999), p. 42.

nothing but the debris of those of our fathers. The same materials that served to form those who are no more, will one day be employed in the composition of those who are not yet. The Lord created, once and for all time, a certain quantity of matter, which is neither increased nor diminished, to which nothing will be added, and over which the void has no more rights. Said matter has been divided into elements. These elements circulate, so to speak, going from the composition of a horse to that of a man, and from the composition of a man to that of a tree, and so on with the rest. It's precisely the juncture of these elements that makes a body; the way they are joined is what makes all the difference between one body and another, and the proportions or the equilibrium, more or less observed in each composition, are uniquely decisive about its duration.

The elements, although made to work together, in all and for all things, nevertheless always tend to destroy each other. The one that dominates in a body soon sows division among the rest, and finally forces them to a separation, the only victim of which is what we call the form; for, matter, that is, the elements, are soon brought together again, although differently from before; just as they destroy each other, they also determine each other. This is the economy of the destructions and productions which happen at every moment, which the ignorant regard as annihilation and creation.

Now, what will the Lord do to render contemporaries so many men, each of whom only had a body because they seem to have taken their time and their measures to pass them along to others? Certainly he won't create new ones. Assuming this, I know of only one expedient, and this expedient, Sir, will do away with our mutual doubts.

If we all resurrect some day, it is clear that our bodies will no longer be subject to the needs of this life, and will no longer feel the intemperance of the climates and seasons; insensitive to cold and heat, we will have no more need of water to refresh and moisten us, or any sun to heat and purify us; freed as we will be from any need to eat, the earth, this liberal and common mother, will become useless to us; the hills, which are the retreats of most of the animals made for the use of mortal man, the mountains, these greedy trustees of the treasures which cupidity makes necessary for us, all of this will also be superfluous among uninterested mortals. The heavens and their luminaries will no longer have to mark the hours for us, and we will have no use for their uneven light in a time when the very author of day will give us light; so that, given the futility of all these things and others contained in space, they must cease to be what they are. The order and harmony of the universe will be overthrown and confounded; everything will universally become a heap of matter again, an unformed mass, a chaos and a confusion, just as it was on the day of the creation.

Don't you believe, Sir, that the Creator will find in all these materials all he needs to make as many men as necessary? And the space you were worried about, will also be in good supply, since even then there will be nothing in the world but that which is contained in it at the present hour. The number of men will be infinitely larger, indeed, but there will also be no more forests, no more buildings, no more mountains, no more boulders, etc. Since all matter will be used only to make men, space will no longer have anything but men to contain. And if, despite all these wise precautions, matter should be lacking, the skilled artisan will make do with forming bodies sparer than your own. In case of need, you can offer the stuff to make four more; to speak in confidence, I don't despair at the idea of seeing you in a shape as fine as what you had formerly. The Duke of Roquelaure will have a nose, and the Duke of Étrées will have only one; and if the minds of a certain order are then as rare as they are in our day, and which is necessarily the case, I know you for your neighbors -- which is not said to frighten you. Nor do I know whether ladies will keep their sex in this universal upheaval, or if it will only be those who lived good lives, to whom the form of a man will be granted. I will inform myself on their fate in the first long conversation I have with my genius; but if what he teaches me is unfavorable to them, don't expect, Sir, that I'll ever tell you the secret.

I have the honor, etc.
FONTENELLE.

ON THE ORIGIN OF THE FABLES

(1684)

We are so strongly habituated during our childhood to the Fables of the Greeks that, when we come to the age of reason, we never realize how astonishing they truly are. But, if we manage to lose the eyes of habit, we will necessarily be spooked to see the entire ancient History of a People, which is only a heap of chimeras, reveries and absurdities. Can it be possible that the whole thing was once considered factual? For what reason would it have been given to us as something false? What was this love of men for manifest and ridiculous falsehoods, and why has it not endured? Because the Greek Fables weren't like our Novels which are seen for what they are, not as Histories; there are no ancient Histories aside from these Fables. Let us seek clarity on this matter, if we can; let's study the human mind in one of its strangest productions: which is so often where it is best revealed.

In the first centuries of the world, and with Nations that either hadn't heard of the Traditions of Seth's family, or who didn't preserve them, ignorance and barbarity must have risen to an excess that we can hardly imagine.

Think of our Kaffirs, the Lapps, or the Iroquois; and let's not forget that these Peoples, who are already ancient, must have attained some degree of knowledge and polish that the first men lacked.

In proportion to one's ignorance and lack of experience, one will see more miracles. The first Men therefore saw many; and since fathers naturally tell their children what they have seen and what they have done, all their stories back then were full of miracles.

When we say something surprising, our imagination warms up to an object, and tends automatically to enlarge and fill in any gaps to make it completely wondrous, as if it felt regret at leaving such a brilliant thing incomplete. In addition, we are flattered by the feelings of surprise and admiration arising in our audience, and want to excite them further, anticipating some additional benefit to our vanity. These two reasons joined together, make a given man, who had no intention to lie when he began telling a somewhat unusual story, might even catch himself lying, if he's being careful; and therefore a kind of effort and close attention is necessary to avoid saying anything but the precise truth. And what does this mean for those who naturally love to invent tales and trick others?

The stories the first Men gave their children, therefore often false in themselves because they were made by men who were subject to see many things that weren't so, and beyond that, having been exaggerated, or in good faith, as we have just explained, or in bad faith, it is clear that they are already quite spoiled at the source. But surely things will be far worse when they pass from mouth to mouth; everyone will take away some little ray of truth, and bring in a falsehood, especially a miraculous kind of falsehood, which is the most pleasant sort; and perhaps after a century or two, not only will nothing remain of the little truth that was there to begin with, but nothing will remain of the first falsehood.

Will I find a hearing for what I'm about to say? There was Philosophy even in these vulgar centuries, and it did much to promote the birth of the Fables. Those who have a little more genius than others are naturally led to seek the causes of what they see. "Where is the source of this ever-flowing river?" A contemplative of those ages must have asked himself. An odd sort of Philosopher, but one who might have been a Descartes in our time. After long meditation, he very happily discovered that there was someone who always took care to pour this water from a jug. But who provided him with this supply of water? The contemplative didn't go this far.

We must realize that these ideas, which can be called the Systems of those days, were always copied according to things that were known better. Water had often been seen poured from jugs: thus it was easy to imagine how a God would pour the water of a River; and due to the ease of imagining this, they were entirely disposed to believe it. Thus, to make sense of Thunder and Lightning, they readily imagined a God in human form shooting fiery upon us; an idea that is manifestly taken from very familiar objects.

This Philosophy of the first turned on a principle that is so natural that even today our Philosophy has none other; that is, that we explain nature's unknown things by those that we have in front of our eyes, and by which we transport to physics the ideas provided to us by experience. We have discovered through use, and not simply guessed, what can be accomplished by weights, springs, levers; we make Nature act only by levers, weights and springs. These poor Savages who originally inhabited the world, either didn't know these things, or gave them no attention. Therefore, they only explained the effects of Nature by the most crude and tangible things they knew. What have we done? We have always represented the unknown in the shape of what we already knew; but fortunately, there is every reason to believe that the unknown can't help but resemble what is presently known to us.

It was from this crude Philosophy, which was necessarily dominant in the first centuries, that the Gods and Goddesses were born. It is rather curious to see how the human imagination has begotten false Deities. Men saw many things they couldn't have done: hurling bolts of lightning, whipping up the winds, agitating the Sea's waves, all this was far above their power. They imagined beings who were more powerful than them, and capable of producing these great effects. These Beings necessarily had to be made like Men; what other shape might they have had? From the moment they assumed human shape the imagination naturally attributed to them all that is human; they were Men in every way, except that they are always a little more powerful than Men.

This is the origin of something which hasn't yet been thought through, which is that, in all the Deities the Pagans dreamed up, the idea of power was always dominant, and little attention was given either to Wisdom, or Justice, or any of the other attributes that follow the Divine Nature. Nothing better proves how ancient these Deities were, or better shows how the imagination has approached their formation. The first Men prized no quality above physical strength; Wisdom and Justice scarcely had names in the ancient Languages, as they still don't among the Barbarians of America: besides, the first idea that men gained of some Superior Being, came from amazing events, not at all the regulated order of the Universe that they were not capable of recognizing or admiring. Thus, they imagined the Gods in a time when they had nothing more desirable to give them than power, and they imagined them on the basis of what showed power, and not what offered wisdom. It is, therefore, no surprise that they would have imagined many Gods, often opposed to each other, cruel, bizarre, unjust, ignorant; none of that goes directly against the idea of force and power, which is the only one they could have used. These Gods necessarily showed, both the times when they were made, and the occasions that produced them. And, what a lowly kind of power were they given! Mars, the God of war, is wounded in a fight with a Mortal: this certainly detracts from his dignity; but in his retreat, he gives a cry as loud as ten thousand men together: this loud shriek gives Mars the advantage over Diomedes; and this is enough, according to judicious Homer, to save the God's honor. Given how the imagination is formed, it is contented with little, and it will always recognize as a Deity whatever has a little more power than a Man.

Cicero said somewhere that he would have preferred to see Homer transferring the qualities of the Gods to men, instead of transferring, as he did, the qualities of men to the Gods. But Cicero was expecting too much; what he in his day referred to as the Gods' qualities were in no way known in Homer's times. The Pagans have always patterned their Deities on themselves: thus, to the extent that Man were perfected, the Gods were too. The first Men are very brutish, and with them everything is based on force: the Gods will be nearly as brutish, and only a little more powerful; thus with the Gods of Homer's age. Men begin to have ideas of Wisdom and Justice: the Gods make the same gains, they begin to be wise and just, and are always more and more so in proportion as these ideas are perfected among men: behold the Gods of the time of Cicero, and they were far better than those of the time of Homer, because far better Philosophers had set their hands to them.

So far the first Men have begotten the Fables, without it being, so to speak, their own fault. They were ignorant, and consequently they saw many miracles: people naturally exaggerate unusual things in the telling thereof, they acquire even more diverse falsehoods when they pass through many mouths; kinds of philosophical Systems are established, which are both crude and absurd, but nothing else is possible. We will now see that on these foundations men have in a way taken pleasure in tricking themselves.

That which we call the Philosophy of the first ages turns out to have been completely fit to be allied with the History of their goings-on. A young Man fell into a river, and nobody could recover his body. What became of him? The Philosophy of the day taught that this River contained young girls who governed it: the young Girls carried the young man off, which is natural enough; this no further evidence is necessary. A Man whose birth is obscure has some extraordinary talent; there are Gods made almost like Men: they cease to look into his parentage; he is the son of one of those Gods. Carefully consider most of the Fables, you'll find that they are only a mixture of facts with the Philosophy of the times, which explained very comfortably what was miraculous in the facts, and married itself to them quite naturally. It was only Gods and Goddesses who were just like us, and who blended in very well on the stage with men.

Since the Histories of true facts mixed with these false imaginations were very prevalent, they began to be forged without any basis; or at least the more remarkable facts were only recounted when dressed up in the ornaments that had been recognized as most pleasant. These ornaments were false, maybe even since they were sometimes presented as such; and yet the Histories weren't considered fabulous. That will become intelligible if we make a comparison with our modern History with the ancient kind.

In times of greater intelligence, as in the age of Augustus and this one, people have loved to reason on the actions of Men, to discover their motives, and to get acquainted with their characters. The Historians of these ages have become accustomed to this taste, they have been careful to write the facts nakedly and dryly; they have accompanied them with motives, and have mixed these with the portraits of their personalities. Do we think that these portraits and motives were the precise truth? Do we have the same faith in these as in the facts? No; we know quite well that the Historians guessed them as well as they could, and that it's nearly impossible for them to have guessed with complete accuracy. However, we don't find it wrong for the Historians to have sought out this embellishment which remains within the bounds of likelihood; and it's due to this likelihood that this mixture of the false which we are aware might be in our Histories, doesn't make us regard them as Fables.

In the same way, after, by the aforementioned means, the ancient Peoples contracted the taste for these Histories which included Gods and Goddesses, and the miraculous in general, Men no longer told Histories without such ornamentation. It was known that that might not be true; but in those days it was plausible, which was enough to preserve for these Fables the quality of Histories.

Even today the Arabs fill their Histories with wonders and miracles, which for the most part are ridiculous and grotesque. No doubt, they regard such as ornamentation, about which nobody worries about being deceived, it being a kind of convention among them to write this way. But when these sorts of Histories pass to other Peoples who have a taste for facts written with exact truthfulness, which is taken literally, or at least they're convinced that they were believed by those who promulgated them, and by those who have accepted them without contest. Certainly the misunderstanding is considerable. When I've said that the falseness of these histories was recognized for what it was, this was in reference to somewhat enlightened peoples; for, as for the Masses, they are destined to be the dupe of everything.

Not only in the first Centuries did men explain with a chimerical Philosophy all that was surprising in the History of the facts; but what pertained to Philosophy was explained by Histories of facts imagined on the spot. They saw in the North two Constellations called the two She-bears, which were always visible and never went to bed like the others; they never dreamed that this is because they were near an elevated Pole with respect to their Spectators, they didn't know that much: they imagined that one of these two She-bears was formerly a Mistress, the other a son of Jupiter; that after these two people had been changed into Constellations, jealous Juno had begged the Ocean not to allow them to descend with it like the others, who go there to rest. All the Metamorphoses are the Physics of these first times. Mulberries are red because they are tinged with the blood of two Lovers; the Partridge always flies near the ground because Daedalus, who had changed into a

Partridge, remembered the fate of his son who had flown too high; and so on with the rest. I have never forgotten that I was told in my childhood that Elderberry trees used to produce grapes that were as delicious as those of the vine; but that the traitor Judas had hung himself on this tree, and its fruits had turned as bad as they now are. This Fable could only have originated after Christianity; and it is of precisely the same species as these ancient metamorphoses collected by Ovid, which is to say that Men have always had an inclination for these sorts of histories. They have the double pleasantness of striking the mind with some marvelous quality, and satisfying the curiosity by the apparent reason that they make some effect natural and well known.

Aside from all these principles peculiar to the birth of the Fables, there have been two other more general ones which have been extremely favorable to them. The first is the right everyone has to invent things similar to those which are commonly accepted, or to push them beyond their consequences. Some extraordinary event will have inspired the belief that God had fallen in love with a Woman; suddenly all the Histories will be filled with lusty Gods. You certainly believe one, so why not another? If the Gods have Children, they love them, they put all their powers to use for them on all occasions; and behold an exhaustible source of wonders which couldn't be called absurd.

The second principle which furthers our errors a great deal is the blind respect for Antiquity. Our Fathers believed this or that; would we claim to be wiser than they were? These two principles together work wonders. One, on the slightest foundation that the weakness of human nature has given, extends a stupidity to infinity; the other one, as slight as its basis may be, preserves it forever. One, because we are already in error, commits us more and more to it; & the other one keeps us from extricating ourselves from it, because we've held onto it for a given time.

This, by all appearances, is what pushed these Fables to the high degree of absurdity that they attained, and what kept it there: for, whatever Nature added directly of its own was neither completely so ridiculous nor is such great quantity; and Men are not so insane that they weren't suddenly able to produce such reveries, believe in them, and take a long time to disabuse themselves of them, unless the two things we've just mentioned were involved.

Let's examine the errors of these Centuries; we will find that the same things have established, spread, and preserved them. It is true that we have not arrived at any absurdity as considerable as the ancient Greek Fables; but this is because we haven't set out from such an absurd starting point. We are as capable as they are to further and preserve our own errors: but fortunately they are not as imposing, because we are illuminated by the rays of the true Religion, and, as I believe, by a few rays of the true Philosophy.

The origin of the Fables is ordinarily attributed to the vivid imagination of the Orientals; as for me, I attribute it to the ignorance of the first men. Place a new People under the Pole, its first Histories will be Fables; and indeed aren't all the ancient Histories of the North full of them? These are nothing but Giants and Wizards. I'm not saying that a bright and burning Sun can't still give minds a final boiling, which perfects their disposition to feed on Fables; but for this all Men have talents that are independent of the Sun. Thus, in all I've just said, I haven't supposed in Men anything but what is common to all, and which must have its effect under the Glacial Zones as it does under the Torrid ones.

I could easily show, if necessary, an astonishing conformity between the Fables of the Americans and those of the Greeks. The Americans sent the souls of those who lived badly into certain muddy and disagreeable Lakes, just as the Greeks sent them to the shores of their Rivers Styx and Acheron. The Americans believed that rain fell when a young girl who was in the clouds playing with her younger brother, had her water-jug broken by him: surely this bears a strong resemblance to these Nymphs of the springs, who poured water from pots? According to the traditions of Peru, the Ynca Manco Guyna Capac, The Sun's Son, found a way, by his eloquence, to draw from the depths of the forests the Local Inhabitants who lived there like Beasts, and made them live under rational Laws. Orpheus did the same for the Greeks, and he was also the Sun's Son: which shows that the Greeks were for a time savages just like the Americans, and that they were taken out of Barbarity by the same means; and that the imaginations of these Peoples, although so distant, agreed in believing that those who had extraordinary talents were the Sons of the Sun. Since the Greeks, with all their wit, when they were still a new People, had no more rationality than the American Barbarians, who were, by all appearances, a new People still when they were discovered by the Spaniards, there is reason to believe that the Americans would eventually have become as rational in their thinking as the Greeks, if they had a chance.

Among the Ancient Chinese we also find the method of the ancient Greeks, of inventing Stories to make sense of natural things. Where do high and low tides come from? You guessed it, they won't consider the pressure of the Moon on our Vortex. It's because a Princess had a hundred children; fifty inhabited the coast of the Sea, and the other fifty lived in the Mountains. Two great Peoples resulted, who often make war on each other. When those who live on the coasts have the advantage over those of the Mountains, and drive them back, this is the high tide; when they are repelled, and run away from the Mountains towards the coast, this is the low tide. This way of philosophizing is quite close to that of Ovid's Metamorphoses; so true it is that the same ignorance has produced nearly the same effects with all Peoples.

This is the reason why there is none whose History doesn't begin with Fables, aside from the chosen People, among whom the special care of Providence has preserved the truth. How amazingly slow men are to arrive at something rational, as simple as it may be! To preserve the memory of things as they were is no great marvel; however, many Centuries would pass before anyone was capable of doing this, and until then the facts that were remembered will only be visions and dreams. It would be quite misguided, therefore, to be surprised that Philosophy and the manner of reasoning should have been so crude and imperfect for so many centuries, and that even today they progress so slowly.

With most Peoples, Fables turn into Religion; but in addition, with the Greeks, they turned, so to speak, into entertainment. Since they provide nothing but ideas fitted to the most common sort of human imagination, Poetry and Painting paired perfectly with it, and we all know how passionate the Greeks were for these fine Arts. Deities of all kinds spread all over, which make everything living and animated, who take an interest in everything, and more importantly, Deities who often act in a surprising manner cannot fail to have a pleasant effect, whether in Poems or in Paintings, where they need only to seduce the imagination by showing it things it can grasp easily, and which capture it at the same time. How could Fables fail to convince it, since they're born from it? When Poetry or Painting have put them to work to put on a show for our imagination, they've done nothing but return its own handiwork to it.

Errors, once established among men, tend to grow deep roots, and to hang onto different things for support. Religion and common sense have disabused us of the Greek Fables; but they are still maintained among us by means of Poetry and Painting, by which they seem to have found a way to make themselves indispensable.

Although we are incomparably more enlightened than those crude minds which candidly invented the Fables, we find it easy to conceive of this same turn of mind that rendered the Fables so pleasant to them; they relished them because they believed in them, while we can enjoy them no less without believing them; and there is no better proof that imagination and reason have nothing to do with each other, and that things which reason has completely discarded lose none of their charm for the imagination.

So far nothing has been introduced into this History of the Origin of the Fables, but what comes from the depths of human nature, and indeed this is what has been dominant in them; but alien things were also brought in, which must also be discussed at this point. For example, since the Phoenecians and the Egyptians were more ancient Peoples than the Greeks, their Fables passed to the Greeks, and were enlarged in transit, and even their truest histories became Fables. The Phoenician Language, and maybe the Egyptian one too, was full of ambiguous words; besides, the Greeks understood neither, and behold a marvelous source of misunderstanding. Two Egyptian women, whose name means Doves, came to live in the Forest of Dodona to tell the future there; the Greeks understood these to be two real Doves perched on trees who prophesied, and then soon after the trees themselves were making prophecies. A Ship's Rudder has a Phoenician name that also means "talking"; the Greeks, in the Story of the Ship Argus, thought that there was a talking Rudder. The Savants of these latter days have found a thousand other examples, which clearly show that the origin of many Fables consists in what is commonly called *qui pro quo*, and that the Greeks were very liable to suffer from these relative to the Phoenecian or Egyptian languages. For my part, I find that the Greeks, for all their intelligence and curiosity, showed a lack of both when they failed to learn these Languages, or neglected them. Did they not know that nearly all their Cities were Colonies of the Egyptians or the Phoenicians, and that most of their ancient histories came from these Countries? Don't the origins of their Language and the Antiquities of their Country depend on these two Languages? But these were barbaric, harsh, and unpleasant Languages. What a funny sort of delicacy!

When the art of writing was invented, this lent itself immensely to spreading the Fables, and enriching one People with all the nonsense coming from another one; but all that was gained was that the uncertainty of the tradition was stabilized somewhat, the growth of the heap of Fables was slowed somewhat, and it remained nearly in the state that obtained when Writing was discovered.

Ignorance gradually diminished, and consequently fewer wonders were seen, men made fewer false systems of Philosophy, the Histories were less like Fables; since all these things are related. Up to that point, they had only retained the memory of past things from sheer curiosity: but it was realized that it might be a useful thing to retain, whether to preserve things which the Nations boasted of, or to be able to judge on the quarrels that might arise between Peoples, or to provide examples of virtue; and I think that this custom was the last one they thought of, although it's the most well known one. All of this required that History had to be true: I mean true by opposition to the ancient Histories, which were filled with nothing but nonsense. They then began to write History in some Nations in a more rational way, which usually offered more plausibility.

Then no new Fables appeared; they were content to preserve the old ones. But what are minds insanely besotted with Antiquity not capable of? They imagine that these Fables conceal the secrets of Physics and Morality. Might it have been possible for the Ancients to have produced such reveries without introducing some subtlety in them? The words "the Ancients" always has an imposing ring to it: but assuredly those who created the Fables weren't the sort of men who were knowledgeable in Morality or Physics, nor could they have discovered the art of disguising them with borrowed images.

We should not, therefore, look for anything in the Fables, but the History of the errors of the human mind. It is less apt for them when it knows just how vulnerable it is. It's not a science to fill one's head with all this nonsense from the Phoenecians and the Greeks; but it is one to know what led the Phoenecians and the Greeks to such extravagance. All men are so similar that there is no People whose idiocy should not make us shiver.

ON THE DIVERSITY OF RELIGIONS

OR,

THE DECEPTIVE MEANS TO WHICH WE FIND OURSELVES COMMITTED BY A MISFORTUNE INDEPENDENT OF US

(1695)[22]

What an astonishing spectacle, this infinite difference of cults which divide the universe! Instructed by all that surrounds them, instructed further by the inner sense of their weakness, men are in agreement to submit to some supreme being, and they all disagree about the idea they form thereof. All that touches our senses, and all that the mind alone can think of, all that is the most brilliant, the most elevated above us, and all that seems lowest; all that is beneficent in nature, and all that is fearsome and dire therein, all of these have been a deity for some people, all has had its incense, its altars and its victims. The diversity of religions has corresponded to that of the deities. In one place they want gods who are always

---

[22] From: Alain Mothu, Alain Sandrier. *Minora clandestina: le philosophe antichrétien et autres écrits iconoclastes de l'âge classique* (Champion, 2003). Reprinted on pages 94ff.

visible, always present with their statues; elsewhere it's a crime to represent the object of worship: in one place blood is shed, either of animals or men; elsewhere it's only the fumes of incense: in one place they use games and spectacles, to appease furious Heaven; elsewhere, they try to sway it with rigorous self-imposed suffering. That which honors the deities of one country would outrage those of another, and the holiest ceremonies of one people are sacrilegious for their neighbors.

However, there is only one God, and a jealous one. Miserable, a hundred times more miserable than we can comprehend, are the nations which pay to other deities the praise which belongs to him alone! Their gods can do nothing for them, and he who can do all is not their god. The honors they pay to one who can do nothing to repay them, are so many insults against the one who can punish them. And what a prodigious, what a countless multitude is enveloped in such a fatal error! Among all the different nations comprising the variety of cults, three peoples alone address their vows and adoration to he who is.

It is not enough even to recognize this unique sovereign of the universe. Three great peoples recognize him, and he rejects two of these. They do not approach him via his son, this adorable son, who has deigned to purchase with all his blood the right to receive all the vows of humanity on his behalf, and to erase the unhappy stain which renders, so to speak, our very birth criminal. As for this son, who alone can lead us to his father, it is not even enough to invoke his name and to implore his aid.

From East to West, numerous churches flatter themselves about their eternal alliance with him, but only one is his bride; all the rest have no portion in his love or his favors.

Among so many diverse religions, among so many different paths, all gruesome, apart from one only, who can show us the unique path which is so important to know? Alas! The one we are dropped into by accident of birth, is nearly always the one thought to be the path of salvation. All the peoples on Earth walk in diverse paths with equal confidence.

How can a first opinion fail to impress men, when it takes them so young, where if finds neither reason to combat, nor alternative views to destroy; which acquires from day to day, by the force of the inhabitants, an ever more unshakable authority; which is sustained by mutual examples of credulity; which is supported by the most illustrious and revered names; which has passed whole centuries in a peaceable reign; which finds proofs in its long duration, and which ultimately can only be attacked at the expense of the honor of an entire nation? How many vast climates, to this day plunged in the darkness of idolatry, ignore even the name of Christianity, or have only what feeble knowledge might come to them across the seas that separate them from us! Or ultimately, if our zeal should bring greater light to these peoples, can they easily dissipate this fog of prejudices, so ingrained and so powerful, which rises without cease against them and obscures their view? The truth appears, but with a new, alien, dangerous aspect, as the enemy of all; and it will be a rather great triumph for it if, under a disadvantageous form, it obtains even the slightest attention.

Within Christianity itself, other peoples have an even more fearsome disposition. They are born, so to speak, enemies of the known truth. Since it must strike them all over, they are armed against it from childhood. They are carefully taught the dreadful art of refusing to submit to it. Their eyes will never be unsealed by any new brilliance that catches them off guard, they are accustomed to it: they will not be affected by the pleas of those who beckon them to the right path; they call them in turn to this path of perdition where they are headed, and the just compassion felt for their error, they return to those who walk in the right path.

O celestial truth! Is it you who gives too little light to men? Is it men who are unable to receive your light? Why is this darkness almost universal on earth? Why is this prodigious multitude of nations, which are running unawares to their certain ruin? Can a single error make them worthy of such an unhappy fate?

Let us not seek beyond the allowed limits into the decrees of the divine providence; let us submit to its laws. God is just, he punishes only the guilty, and even when the rigors of his justice seem excessive to us, let us be sure that if they were reduced, the supreme reason would suffer thereby. All men are offshoots from a criminal stem, they are all born children of wrath: woe to those to whom God refuses what he does not owe them at all! Once again let us be submissive, and if our feeble reason gave us different views, let us prefer a salutary ignorance over these dangerous views.

AN ACCOUNT OF THE ISLAND OF BORNEO

(1686)

AN EXTRACT FROM A LETTER WRITTEN FROM BATAVIA IN THE EAST INDIES

Written from Batavia, in the East Indies, on 27 November 1684.[23]

Dear sir,

You know that on the Island of Borneo, which is our neighbor, only women have claim to royalty. Those People are so wary of being governed by those who are truly of Royal Blood, and they have such an opinion of female fragility, that they must always have a Queen whose children belong to her without any doubt; and for the utmost security, the most important men of the Country must be present when their Queens give birth. A few years ago Queen Mliseo died, and her daughter Mreo succeeded her, recognized from the start in all the Island without difficulty. The beginning of her reign was

---

[23] Published in Pierre Bayle's *Nouvelles de la République des Lettres*, Jan. 1686.

agreeable to her Subjects, but soon the novelties she gradually introduced into the Government led many to murmur. Mreo wanted all her Ministers to be Eunuchs, a very harsh condition, and which had never been imposed to that point, and yet she only had them mutilated in a certain way which didn't keep the husbands from bemoaning them. It's the Queen's custom to hold public festivals for their Subjects on set days. Mreo had cut back on half of what the other Queens had given; beyond which, in her reign, bread was excessively dear in the whole Island, & nobody knew what had happened to it; except that certain Magicians in her pay were accused of making it perish with their words. There was also much complaining about certain newly constructed prisons where she had criminals cast, and from which she took them if a price was paid, which increased her revenues considerably. But nothing was more jarring to the Inhabitants of Borneo than the hall of cadavers in the Queen's Palace, although in reality this wasn't a serious problem for her Subjects. She had the bodies of her Favorites embalmed when they died, they were arranged in this hall with great formalities, and one had to pay one's respects to them before entering the chambers of Mreo. There were some naturally proud and independent minds that were unable to resolve themselves to do so. The people of the Island were therefore very unhappy with the Government, when a new Queen appeared, who claimed to be the daughter of Mliseo, and to dispossess Mreo. She began by abolishing all the novelties the masses were complaining about; no eunuchs for her, no Magicians raising the price of bread, no halls for any cadavers, no prisons according to the former order, no imperfect festivals. I forgot to mention that the people of Borneo hold the opinion that legitimate children should resemble their parents. Eenegue (the name of the new Princess) looked exactly like the late Queen Mliseo; whereas Mero had almost no feature in common with her: thus it was noticed that Mreo didn't like showing herself in public; it's even said that she had destroyed, as far as she could, the portraits of Mliseo. Eenegue, on the contrary, preserved them with all her might, and focused mostly on her resemblance. Mreo had also, for her part, a great advantage, that she had so obviously been born of Mliseo, at least by the report of the Gentlemen who were supposed to have acted as witnesses, and these gentlemen hadn't seen Eenegue's birth. It is true that Eenegue claimed that they had been corrupted; which was far from plausible. She also told a history of her birth, by which she turned out to be the legitimate Daughter of Mliseo, but this story was nearly unbelievable, and almost like that of Count Saint-Geran, so famous in Europe. However, the contestation of these two Queens divided the whole Island, and caused wars everywhere. Some hold to resemblance against the certainty of birth, others for the certainty of birth against resemblance. Many blood-soaked battles have taken place, and none of the parties has completely ruined the other. It's thought however that Mreo will be victorious. It's not long since she ambushed a part of the Army of Eenegue in very difficult places, and demanded oaths of faithfulness. If her party doesn't receive extraordinary new forces, because her soldiers don't fight all that willingly under its banners, at least Enegue has suffered greatly. I'll make a note to teach you, next year, how this war turned out, since you love history enough not to neglect that of these barbarous lands, whose morals and customs are so strange.

I have the honor, etc.

A TREATISE ON LIBERTY

IN FOUR PARTS.

(1690s)

FIRST PART

In relation to the free acts of men, human liberty and God's foreknowledge are always assumed, and the difficulty is thought to reside only in harmonizing the two things.

However, neither of them has been proved, and it may even be that some are perplexed by such a question, the parts of which are untrue. I will look at the bigger picture, and examine, first, whether God can foresee actions of free causes, and second, whether men perform them.

On the first question, I say that I call foreknowledge all knowledge of the future. The nature of God's foreknowledge is unknown to me; but I know something about human foreknowledge, by which I can judge about God's, since it is common to God and all men.

The Astronomers infallibly predict Eclipses; God also predicts them.

This foreknowledge of God and this foreknowledge of the Astronomers about the Eclipses agree in the fact that both God and the Astronomers conceive of a necessary and invariable order in the movement of the celestial bodies, and that they consequently predict the Eclipses which are part of that order.

These kinds of foreknowledge differ, firstly, in that, in the celestial movements, God understands the order which he himself established, and that the Astronomers are not the Authors of the order they can understand.

Secondly, in that God's foreknowledge is entirely precise, and that that of the Astronomers is not; because the lines of celestial motion are not as regular as they assume, and their observations cannot be entirely correct.

No other agreements or differences can be found.

In order for the Astronomers' foreknowledge about Eclipses to be equal to God's, all it would take is to remove these differences.

The first, per se, is of no importance. It doesn't matter if someone established an order to predict its workings, it's sufficient to understand this order as perfectly as if one had made it oneself, and although a person can't be its

Author without knowing it, they can know it without being its Author.

In effect, if foreknowledge were only found where power is found, there would be no foreknowledge for the Astronomers about the celestial movements, since they have no power over this. Therefore, God doesn't have foreknowledge in his quality as the Author of all things, but he does have it in his quality as a being who understands the order inherent in all things.

It only remains, then, to remove the second difference between the foreknowledge of God and that of the Astronomers. For this, all it takes is to post the Astronomers as being perfectly informed about the irregularities of the celestial movements and as having made entirely precise observations. There is nothing absurd in this assumption.

On this condition, then, it could be claimed, without any temerity, that the foreknowledge of Astronomers about Eclipses would be precisely equal to that of God in terms of simple foreknowledge.

Therefore, the foreknowledge of God about eclipses would not extend to things where that of the Astronomers could not reach.

And yet, it's certain that, as capable as the Astronomers were, they could not foresee the eclipses, if the Sun or Moon might sometimes stray from their paths independently of any given cause and of all the rules.

Therefore, nor could God foresee the eclipses; and this lack of foreknowledge in God would have the same cause as the lack of foreknowledge of the Astronomers.

But the Astronomers' lack of foreknowledge wouldn't be due to the fact that they aren't the Authors of the celestial movements, since that has nothing to do with foreknowledge, nor with the fact that they don't know the movements well enough, since we're supposing that they know them as well as is possible; but their lack of foreknowledge would be due only to the fact that the established order in the celestial movements isn't necessary and invariable: therefore, the same God's lack of foreknowledge has the same cause.

Therefore God, although infinitely powerful and infinitely intelligent, can never foresee that which doesn't depend on a necessary and invariable order.

Therefore, God doesn't foresee the actions from what are called free causes.

Therefore, there are no free causes, whose actions God doesn't foresee.

In effect, it's easy to conceive that God infallibly foresees everything relating to the physical order of the universe, because this order is necessary and subject to the invariable rules which he has established. This is the principle of his foreknowledge.

But, on what principles could he foresee the actions of a cause which nothing could determine by necessity? The second principle of foreknowledge, which must be different from the first, is absolutely inconceivable; and since we have one which is easy to conceive, it is more natural and consistent with the idea of the simplicity of God to believe that this principle is the only one on which all his foreknowledge is based.

It is not part of God's greatness to foresee things which he himself would have made unpredictable.

SECOND PART

We must not, therefore, take liberty from men to save a universal foreknowledge for God; but first we must know if man is actually free.

Let us examine this second question in itself and on these essential principles, without even considering the prejudice of our opinion of our own liberty, and without worrying about the consequences. Here are my thoughts.

That which is dependent on something has a certain proportionality with this thing, that is, it receives changes when it receives them, according to the nature of their proportions.

That which is independent of something has no proportionality with it, so that it remains the same when it takes on increases and diminutions.

I assume, along with all Metaphysicians, 1) That the soul thinks according to the way the brain is disposed, and that all the soul's thoughts correspond to certain material arrangements of the brain, and to certain motions which occur there. 2) That all the objects, even the spiritual ones, about which one thinks, leave material dispositions, that is, traces in the brain. 3) I also assume a brain containing two simultaneous material dispositions, which are opposites and equally strong; the first of which lead the soul to think virtuously about a certain subject, the second of which lead it to think viciously.

This hypothesis cannot be refused. The opposing material dispositions can easily come together in the brain to the same degree, and they even necessarily meet whenever the soul deliberates and doesn't know how to decide.

Assuming this, I say: either the soul can absolutely determine, in this equilibrium, the dispositions of the brain to choose between the virtuous and vicious thoughts, or it cannot absolutely determine itself in this equilibrium.

If it can determine itself, it has within itself the power of self-determination, since in its brain everything tends only to indecision, and yet it determines itself.

Therefore, this power which it has of self-determination is independent of the dispositions of the brain.

Therefore, it has no proportionality with them.

Therefore, it remains the same, although they change.

Therefore, if the brain's equilibrium holds, the soul determines itself to think virtuously, it will retain the power of self-determination if the material disposition to think viciously prevailed.

Therefore, no matter how high this material disposition to vicious thoughts might rise, the soul would have no less power to determine itself to the choice of virtuous thoughts.

Therefore, the soul has within itself the power of self-determination, despite all the opposite dispositions of the brain.

Therefore, in the first case, the thoughts of the soul are always free. Let us proceed to the second case.

If the soul cannot determine itself absolutely, this comes only from the supposed equilibrium in the brain; and clearly it will never make a choice until one of these dispositions defeats the other, and it is necessarily determined in favor of the triumphant one.

Therefore, its power of determining itself to the choice of virtuous or vicious thoughts is absolutely dependent on the dispositions of the brain.

Therefore, in the second case, the soul does not have any power of self-determination of itself, and the dispositions of the brain are what make it choose vice or virtue.

Therefore, the thoughts of the soul are never free.

Thus, by comparing the two cases, we find that the thoughts of the soul are always free, or that they are never free in any case whatsoever.

But, it is true and universally recognized that the thoughts of children, of those who are dreaming, of those who suffer from fevers, and madmen, are never free.

The crux of this argument is easy to see. It sets up a principle, which is uniform in the soul, so that the principle is always either independent of the dispositions of the brain, or always dependent on them; whereas, as is commonly thought, it's dependent sometimes, and independent at other times.

It's said that the thoughts of those with fevers and madmen are not free, because the material dispositions of the brain are so attenuated and elevated that the soul can't resist them; whereas in the healthy, the dispositions of the brain are moderated and don't necessarily overpower the soul.

But firstly, in this system, since the principle is not uniform, it must be abandoned, if I can explain everything by one which is.

Secondly, if a weight of five pounds could fail to be overcome by a weight of six pounds, then clearly, not even a thousand pounds would make any difference; for if it resisted the six pounds because of some principle independent of weight, and this principle, whatever it was, would have no more proportionality with a weight of a thousand pounds than with one of six, because it would be of a completely different nature from that of weight.

Therefore, if the soul resists a material disposition of the brain which leads it to choose vice, and which, although moderated, is still stronger than the material disposition to virtue, then the soul must resist the same material disposition to vice, if it is infinitely above its opposite, because it can only have resisted it initially by a principle independent of the dispositions of the brain, and which must not change because of the dispositions of the brain.

In third place, if the soul could see clearly despite a disposition of the eye which weakened its sight, we could conclude that it could still see in spite of a disposition of the eye which completely obstructed its vision, as a material phenomenon.

In fourth place, it's agreed that the soul depends absolutely on the dispositions of the brain as to the degree of intelligence; but if, relative to virtue or vice the dispositions of the brain only determine the soul in extreme quantities, and they leave it free when moderated, so there can be plenty of virtue despite a moderate disposition to vice, it should also be possible to have plenty of intelligence despite a moderate disposition to stupidity, which cannot be allowed. It is true that effort can increase one's intelligence, or rather, it strengthens the dispositions of the brain, and thus the mind grows precisely as the brain is perfected.

In fifth place, I assume that the only difference between a brain which is awake and a sleeping brain is that a sleeping brain is less filled with spirits, and that the nerves are less tense, so that the motions are not communicated from one nerve to another, and the spirits which reopen one trace don't reopen another which is connected to it.

Assuming this, if the soul has the power to resist the dispositions of the brain when they are weak, it is always free during dreams, where the dispositions of the brain, which lead it to certain things, are always quite weak. If the reply is given that this is because the only kind of thoughts presented to it offer no matter for deliberation, I would offer the example of a dream where someone deliberates whether or not to kill a friend, which can only be produced by given, opposing material dispositions of the brain; and in this case it seems that, according to the principles of common opinion, the soul should be free.

Now suppose that the person awakens, having decided to kill their friend, and that once awake, they no longer want to kill them: the only change that occurs in the brain is that it has been flooded with spirits, the nerves have tensed. We must see how this produces liberty.

The material disposition of the brain which, in my dream, made me want to kill my friend, was stronger than its opposite number. I say, either the change that occurred in my brain strengthened both of them equally, or they remain in the same disposition they previously had, the first remaining, for example, three times stronger than its opposite; and you couldn't conceive why the soul is free when one of these dispositions has ten degrees of force and the other thirty, and why it isn't free when one of these dispositions has only one degree of force and the other only three.

If this change in the brain has strengthened only one of these dispositions, in order to prove liberty, it must be the one against which I determine myself, that is, the one which led me to want to kill my friend, and then you won't be able to conceive why the force which overcomes this vicious disposition is necessary to enable me to determine myself in favor of the virtuous disposition which remains the same: this change looks more like an obstacle to liberty. Finally, if it strengthens one disposition more than another, it must be the vicious disposition again, and you'll be in no better position to conceive why the force which supervenes on it is necessary for the one to embrace the other, which is always weaker, although stronger than before.

It may also be said that what hinders the liberty of the soul during sleep is the fact the thoughts aren't presented to it with sufficient clearness and distinction. I would respond that the lack of clearness and distinction in thoughts can only keep the soul from knowingly determining itself; but that it can't keep it from determining itself freely, and that it shouldn't take its liberty away, but only the credit or discredit for the decision one makes.

The obscurity and confusion of thoughts means that the soul doesn't know much about what it deliberates on; but it doesn't mean the soul isn't necessarily carried to a decision; otherwise, if the soul were necessarily carried, it would surely be led by those of its thoughts which were least obscure and confused, and I would ask why greater clarity and distinction in thoughts would necessarily determine it while asleep but not while awake, and I would point to all my arguments about the material dispositions.

It seems then that the common principle, which is thought uneven, and both dependent and independent of the brain's dispositions, is subject to insurmountable difficulties, and that it would be better to establish the principle by which the soul determines itself to be always dependent on the dispositions of the brain in every case.

That is more consistent with Physics; according to which it seems that the state of wakefulness, or that of sleep, a passion or a hot fever, childhood and advanced age, really only differ in quantitative terms, and that they shouldn't, consequently, constitute an essential difference, such as granting the soul its liberty, or otherwise.

THIRD PART

The most considerable difficulties in this opinion are the power one has over one's thoughts, and on voluntary movements of the body.

It's commonly agreed that the first thoughts are always presented involuntarily by external objects, or, as amounts to the same thing, by the internal dispositions of the brain: that is quite true. But if the soul formed a first thought independently of the brain, it would also form the second one, and then all the rest, and that, no matter what condition the brain might be in. But it's commonly said that, after the first one was necessarily presented to the soul, the soul has the power to suppress or to strengthen it, to make it cease or continue.

This power is not yet entirely independent of the brain; since, for example, in a dream, the soul might therefore dispose at will of the thoughts which the brain's dispositions offer it. But the common opinion is that, in states of wakefulness or health, the soul has in its brain spirits on which it can imprint, at will, movements meant to suppress or fortify the thoughts which arise, originally, independently of it.

On that, I note that the action of the spirits depends on three things, the nature of the brain on which they act, their own nature, and the quantity, or determination of their movement.

Of these three things, strictly speaking, only the third one can be mastered by the soul. Therefore, the mere power to move spirits is sufficient for liberty.

Yet, I say firstly that, if this power of moving spirits is sufficient to make the soul free as to virtue or vice, though it be master neither of the nature of the brain, nor of that of the spirits, why would it be insufficient to make the soul free with respect to the varying degrees of knowledge and of the natural understanding? If the nature of my brain and of my spirits set me up to be stupid, wouldn't the mere power of guiding the movement of my spirits enable me to have, at will, as much discernment and penetration as I could want?

Secondly, if the power of guiding the motions of the spirits is insufficient for liberty, since the soul must have this power in children, and yet it is unfree, whatever keeps it from being free can only be the nature of its brain, and possibly also that of its spirits.

In third place, why isn't the soul of the insane man free, since it can also direct the movement of its spirits? This power is independent of the dispositions of the brains of the insane. If the reply is that the natural movement of their spirits is then too violent, it follows that, in this state, the forces of the soul have no proportionality with that of the spirits, which necessarily overcome it, but only in a more moderate state where the soul begins to have some proportionality with that of the spirits, the soul cannot completely change the movement of the spirits, but only give them a composite of what they started with and what it freshly imprints on them, which is such a diminution of the soul's liberty; and that ultimately the soul is only completely free when it imprints a movement on the spirits, which had none of themselves: which seems never to happen.

Fourthly, the soul should never find it easier to guide the movement of the spirits than during sleep, and consequently it should never be more free.

If it's replied that the thoughts, the first as well as the second, depend absolutely on the dispositions of the mind, but that they are only the subject-matter of the deliberations, and that the choice the soul makes about it is absolutely free, I ask what causes this difference in nature between the thoughts and the choice one makes between them, and why the insane and sleepers don't make choices that are free and independent of the thoughts to which their brain determines them?

On the body's voluntary movements, the common view is that one moves one's foot or arm freely, and it is true that these movements are voluntary; but it doesn't absolutely follow from this that they are free. That which one does because one wishes to, is voluntary, but it is not free, unless one can really or effectively keep oneself from wanting it. When I move my hand to write, I write because I want to, and if I didn't want to, I wouldn't write; that is voluntary and involves no compulsion. But there is in my brain a material disposition which makes me want to write, so that I can't truly not wish to do so; that is necessary and has nothing free in it; so, that which is voluntary is at the same time necessary, and that which is without liberty doesn't have to involve compulsion.

Conceive then, that, as the brain moves the soul, so that, upon its movement, there is a corresponding thought in the soul, the soul moves the brain, so that, upon its thought there is a corresponding movement of the brain.

The soul is necessarily determined by its brain to want what it wants, and its will necessarily stimulates in its brain a movement by which it brings it to execution.

Thus, if I had no soul I would not do what I do, and if I didn't have such a brain, I wouldn't want to do it.

All the other movements, like that of the heart, etc., are not caused by the soul; it can only operate by means of thought, and whatever is not the effect of a thought, doesn't come from it.

On this principle, I can easily satisfy all that relates to the voluntary motions; but I would like, while using this as a response, to also draw new proofs from it.

I posit a madman who wants to kill someone, and who actually kills him. The movement of this madman's arm is voluntary, that is, produced by the soul, because it wants it; for otherwise, the same material disposition of the brain which had led the madman's soul to want to kill, would also make the spirits flow in the nerves so as to move the arm, and that which had made him want to, must at the same time have executed its will, without the soul's involvement, having impressed no movement on the brain. From which it obviously follows, 1) That if the madman were a pure living machine with no thinking soul, he would still have killed this man even while arming himself for it, and while aiming at his victim, intent on doing harm.

In second place, if this madman were cured, he might still kill a man while wanting to kill him, but without killing him precisely because he wanted to, since the dispositions of the brain which make him want to kill, might yet stimulate in his arm the movement by which it would kill, independently of the soul; in this way, the soul in all men wouldn't be the cause of any motion, but it would only want it when it occurred; and consequently, by removing the soul from the picture, men would still do everything they do, which cannot be affirmed.

Therefore, the movement of this madman's arm is voluntary; but certainly this movement is not free.

Therefore, it is not absolutely of the nature of voluntary movements to be free.

In effect, it's the soul of this madman that moves his arm because it wants to kill; but it is necessarily led to want to kill by the dispositions of his brain.

FOURTH PART

All that remains for me is to discover the source of the universal error about liberty and the cause of our internal feeling.

All prejudices have some basis; and once we find it, we must also discover why we have fallen into error instead of the truth.

The two sources of our error about liberty are that people only do what they want to do, and they often deliberate whether to do it or not.

A slave doesn't think he's free, because he senses that he does what he does in spite of himself, and he sees the external cause which makes him do it; but he would think he was free if it were possible to hide his master from him, and make him carry out his orders without knowing it, and if these orders were always consistent with his inclinations.

Men are in this very condition; they don't know that their brain's dispositions produce all their thoughts and all their diverse wishes; and the orders they receive, so to speak, from their brain are always consistent with their inclinations, since they also cause these inclinations. Thus, the soul thinks it is self-determining, because it was ignorant of and completely unaware of the foreign principle of its determination.

People know that they do all they want to do, but they don't know why they want to; only Physicians can figure that out.

Secondly, one has deliberated, and because one has felt torn between wanting and not wanting, they have thought, after coming to a decision, that they might have made a different one. This conclusion was mistaken; for, something else might have supervened to break the parity between the two choices, which would necessarily have led to a choice. But, they don't realize this, since they had no sense of what had supervened again and resolved their irresolution; and for lack of this feeling, they were led to believe that the soul had decided of its own accord, and independently of any external cause.

What produces this deliberation, and what most people have failed to see, is the equality of forces inherent between two opposing mental dispositions, and which brings opposing thoughts to the soul. As long as this equality subsists, deliberation will occur; but, as soon as one of the material dispositions defeats the other due to some physical cause, the corresponding thoughts are strengthened and become a choice. This is why people often make decisions without any new thoughts, but only because they think something more powerfully than they did before: this is also why people can make decisions without knowing why. If the soul were self-determining, it should always know the reason why. In a wakeful state, the brain is full of spirits and the nerves are tensed, so that motions are communicated from one trace to another which is connected to it. Just as you have only ever heard of homicide described as a crime; when someone makes you think of it, the same movement of the spirits will reopen the traces which represent the horror of this deed to you; and in brief, on any given subject, all the traces connected to it reopen and consequently bring you all the different thoughts which might be entailed by it. But during sleep, the lack of spirits and the relaxation of the nerves set the spirits in motion, which reopen, for example, the traces which make you think of a homicide, don't necessarily reopen those which are connected to it, and which represented it to you as a crime; and, generally speaking, you're not presented with all that you might be able to think about every subject. This is why people think they are free while they're awake, and not while sleeping, even though in both states the soul is equally determined by the dispositions of the brain.

Nobody thinks that insane people are free, since all the dispositions of their brains are so strong about certain things, that they have none at all, or what they do have is infinitely weak, which leads them to contrary things, and consequently, they have no power of deliberation; whereas, in those of a sound mind, the brain is in a certain equilibrium which produces deliberation.

But it's obvious that a weight of five pounds, overcome by a weight of six, is also necessarily overcome by a weight of a thousand pounds, although less quickly; thus, those of a sound mind, determined by a mental disposition which is only a little stronger than its opposite number, are as necessarily determined as those who are pulled along by a disposition which has not been shaken by any other one. But, some are far less impetuous than others, and it seems that impetuosity has been mistaken for necessity, and the softness of the movement for liberty. Men certainly have distinguished the impetuosity or gentleness of the movements from their inner sense; but necessity or liberty can only be decided on through reason.

As to morality, this system makes virtue a pure happiness, and vice a pure misery, it therefore destroys the vanity and all the temerity that virtue can inspire, and leads to a great deal of pity for the wicked, but without inspiring hatred for them. In no way does it remove the hope of correcting them; since with exhortation and example, it's possible to fill their brains with dispositions which will lead them to virtue; and this is what preserves the laws, punishments and rewards.

Criminals are monsters who must be suppressed while mourning for them; their sacrifice frees society from them, and terrifies those who might want to imitate them.

Our good qualities, or the inclination to good, comes from our temperament only, and we must not attribute it to a certain reason, the extreme weakness of which we can recognize.

Those who have the good fortune of being able to work on themselves can strengthen their natural dispositions to good.

Finally, this system changes nothing in the order of the world, except maybe that it takes from good men a reason for honoring themselves and despising others, and helps them suffer insults without feelings of indignation or bitterness for their perpetrators. I do confess that the idea men have of being able to refrain from vice is something which often helps us restrain ourselves, and that the truth we have just discovered is dangerous for those with bad inclinations. But this is not the only place where it seems that God wanted to hide from the majority truths which might harm them.

In addition, this system is very uniform and its principle is very simple, the same thing is decisive for the natural mind and for morals; and, according to the different degrees it receives, it's what distinguishes the madmen from the sages, those who sleep from those who are awake, etc.

Everything is contained within a physical order, in which human actions are, with respect to God, the same thing as eclipses, and where he foresees both things on the same principle.

Haec refutando transcripsi digniori modo sentiens de libertate.

ON HAPPINESS

(1690s)

This is the most important of all subjects, which everyone speaks of, which the philosophers, especially the ancients, have treated at great length: but, as interesting as it may be, its deeper aspects are quite neglected; although everyone talks about it, few think about it; and although the philosophers have treated it copiously, their treatment has been so philosophical that nobody gets any benefit.

Here the word happiness refers to a state, a situation the long duration of which would be desired without any change; and in this way, happiness is different from pleasure, which is only a pleasant feeling, but which is short and passing, and can never constitute a state. Pain would have more of a right to be one.

Measuring the happiness of men only by the number and intensity of the pleasures they have enjoyed during the course of their life, there may be a rather large number of conditions that are rather equal, although very different. He who has fewer pleasures feels them more intensely: he feels an infinity that others no longer feel or never have done; and in this respect nature does its duty well as our common mother. But if, instead of considering these instants scattered throughout the life of each man, we take a profound look at the lives themselves, we see things as very unequal; that a man who has, if you like, during his day as many good moments as anyone else, is far less easy all the rest of the time, and that he receives no compensation whatsoever.

It is, therefore, the state that makes the happiness: but this is very vexatious to humanity. An infinity of men are in a state they are right to dislike; a nearly equal number are incapable of finding contentment in any state at all: they are, therefore, nearly all excluded from happiness, and all that remains for them is pleasures, that is, moments scattered here and there against a background of sadness, who will be cheered up a little by them. Men in these moments regain the forces necessary for their unhappy situation, and are restored for further suffering.

He who would fix his state, not from fear of being worse off, but because he would like to be contented, would like to deserve the title "happy": he would be recognized among all other men by a kind of immobility in his situation; it would only be a case of preserving it, and not departing from it. But has such a man appeared anywhere on earth? This is doubtful, because we never notice those which are in this happy immobility; whereas the more active wretches compose this whirlwind of society, and make themselves all too well known to each other by their violent clashes. Even the repose of the happy, when observed, might look forced, and all others have an interest in forming no better idea of it. Thus, the existence of the happy man might be just as easy to contest. But let's accept it, if only for the sake of our pleasant hopes: but it is true that, kept within certain bounds, they will not be chimerical.

No matter what these proud Stoics may say, a large part of our happiness doesn't depend on us. If one of them, suffering from gout, addressed it as follows: "I refuse to confess that you're an evil"; he's said the most nonsensical word that ever came from the mouth of a philosopher. An emperor of the universe, shut away in a lunatic asylum, naively declares an opinion which he has the misfortune of being imbued with; the former, from commitment to a system, denies a very sharp feeling, and also confesses it by his efforts to deny it. Let's not add to all the evils that nature and fortune might send our way, the absurdity and useless vanity of thinking ourselves invulnerable.

It would be less irrational to convince ourselves that our happiness is completely independent of us; and nearly all men either believe this or act as if they do. Incapable of discernment and choice, pressed along by a blind impetuosity, attracted by objects they only see through a thousand clouds, dragged by each other without knowing where they're going, they compose a confused and tumultuous multitude, which seems to have no other intention than to twist and turn without cease. If, amid all this disorder, favorable encounters might make some of them happy for a few moments, it is quite certain that they will be unable either to prevent or moderate the impact of all the things that could make them unhappy. They are absolutely at the mercy of chance.

We can do something for our own happiness, but only in the way we think; and it must be conceded that this condition is quite hard. Most people only think as would please all those around them; they lack a certain rudder that could turn their thoughts away from the current. Others have thoughts that are so powerfully bent the wrong way, and are so inflexible, that it would be futile to try turning them any other way. Finally some, for whom this labor might lead to success, and would even be quite easy, reject it, because of the effort involved, and scorn the fruit they think is too mediocre. What, then, might this miserable artificial happiness be, for which we would have to cogitate so hard? Is it worth the trouble of tormenting ourselves? We can leave it to the philosophers with their other chimeras: so much study for the sake of happiness would keep anyone from being happy.

Thus, only a part of our happiness can depend on us; and of this small part few are they who have the aptitude or benefit from it. Personalities who are either weak and lazy, or impetuous and violent, or somber and sorrowful, must renounce it. And there are some, gentle and moderate, who more willingly accept pleasant ideas or impressions: they can make fruitful efforts to make themselves happy. It is true that by the grace of nature they are already quite happy, and that the assistance of philosophy doesn't seem entirely necessary for them; but it is almost always for those only who need it least; and they don't cease to feel its importance: especially when happiness is at stake, we must not neglect anything.

Therefore, let us give an ear to philosophy, which preaches in the wilderness to a small troop of selected hearers, because they already knew a good part of what it can teach them.

If the feeling of happiness would enter the soul, or at least sojourn there, we need to clean the place, and drive out all the imaginary evils. We are infinitely skilled at creating these; and once we have produced them, it is very hard for us to get rid of them. It often seems that we love our unhappy production, and take pleasure in it. The imaginary evils are not only those with no physical component, which are only in the mind; but only those that originate in some incorrect, or at least problematic, way of thinking. Dishonor is not an imaginary evil; but the pain of leaving great wealth after one's death to heirs, of indirect lineage instead of one's own, or to daughters instead of sons, clearly is. Some men's lives are poisoned by this sort of sorrow. Happiness does not live in heads of this make; it requires those that are naturally healthier, or those with the courage to heal themselves. If one is vulnerable to imaginary evils, there are so many that they will fall prey to one or another. The principal force of these sorts of monsters consists in the fact that one submits to them, without daring either to attack or even look at them: if they were considered for a while with a steady gaze, they would be half-defeated already.

Quite often we add imaginary circumstances to very real evils, which only aggravate them. If some misfortune has anything unusual about it, not only does its real part upset us, but its uniqueness irritates and embitters us.

We imagine a fortune, a destiny, I know not what, which very artfully and wittily brings us misfortune of a particular nature. But what of all that? If we will use our reason a little, and these phantoms will vanish. A common sort of misery is not really anything less; an unusual misery is no less possible, or less inevitable. Is a man with the plague, its hundred thousandth victim, any less pitiful than someone with a bizarre and unknown disease?

It is true that common misfortunes are foreseen; and this alone softens the idea of death, the greatest of all evils. But who keeps us from foreseeing in general what we call unusual misfortune? Comets can't be predicted like eclipses: but it's safe to say that, from time to time, comets must appear; and so we don't need to worry about them. Unusual misfortunes are rare; and yet, we must expect them to some degree: nearly everyone has those of their own: and if necessary, their designation as unusual could be rightly contested.

An imaginary circumstance we enjoy adding to our afflictions is to believe that we will be inconsolable. Not that this conviction itself isn't sometimes a kind of sweet consolation; surely it is one in the pains in which we might glory, as in the feeling of losing a friend. Then, to believe oneself inconsolable is to demonstrate that one is tender, faithful, constant; it's high praise for oneself. But in those ills where vanity doesn't endure affliction, and where an eternal pain would have no merit, let us be careful not to believe that it must be eternal. We are not perfect enough to be forever suffering: our nature is too variable, and this imperfection is one of its greatest resources.

Thus, before the evils come, they must be foreseen, at least in general; when they have come, we must anticipate some consolation from them. The former softens the blow; the latter shortens the duration of the feeling: we expect what we suffer; and this at least spares us a kind of impatience, a secret revolt which only embitters the pain: we expect not to suffer very long; and then we preempt this time which will be happier, we move ahead.

As for the real circumstances of our evils, we take pleasure in emphasizing these to ourselves, listing them off, as if we sought justice from some judge for an offence we'd suffered. We augment the evil by applying our sight it too much, and by carefully seeking all that might increase it.

We feel a certain complacency for the sharp pains which resists all remedy and refuses all consolation. The tenderest consoler seems indifferent and unpleasant. We would like anything that comes near to take on the feeling that has us in its possession; and any failure to be absorbed like we are, is a kind of offense: above all, those who are audacious enough to question the motives behind our suffering, are our declared enemies. Should we not, on the contrary, be delighted that someone is helping us see falseness and error in the ways of thinking that cause us so much suffering?

Finally, although it is very strange to say so, it remains true that we have a certain love for pain, and that with some characters this is an invincible trait. The first step towards happiness would be to get rid of these, to prune from our imagination all its pernicious talents, or at least to consider it strongly suspicious. Those who are unable to doubt whether they have always had a sound view of everything, are incurable; it is only right that a lesser opinion of oneself should sometimes be rewarded.

Might there be no way of bringing more good than evil from things, and so disposing one's imagination as to sift the pleasures from the sorrows, and let only pleasures in? This proposition is as hard as the philosopher's stone; and if it can be effectuated, it will only be with the happiest nature on earth, and all the art of philosophy. Let's think that most things are of a very doubtful nature; and that, although they strike us very quickly as good or bad, we don't truly know what they are. Some event seemed disastrous when it happened, but later on you would have been unhappy if hadn't occurred; and if you had known what was trailing behind it, you would have absolutely delighted. And, on this footing, how you must regret your sorrowing? We must therefore not rush to be sorry for ourselves: let's wait until what seems so horrible has time to develop. But, on the other hand, that which seems pleasant to us can also bring, can also hide something terrible, and we must not rush to rejoice. This doesn't follow; we shouldn't be as strict about joy as our sorrow.

A great obstacle to happiness is to the expectation of too much happiness. Do we imagine that, before bringing us into the world, we were shown what was prepared for us, and this infinite number of ills that must be distributed among its inhabitants? How terrified wouldn't we have been at the sight of this horrible share that must fall to us? And wouldn't we consider it immense good luck to be free of it at such low cost as one enjoys in these middling conditions, which presently seem unbearable to us? Slaves, those who lack the wherewithal to live, those who live only by the sweat of their brow, those who languish in the habitual maladies; this describes a large part of humanity. What has kept us from such a position? Let's learn how dangerous it is to be men, and consider all the misfortunes from which we are exempt as so many perils from which we have escaped.

An infinity of things we have but never think about, would make someone else supremely happy: the highest dreams of some men is simply to have two arms. It isn't these sorts of goods, which are only goods because their loss would be a great evil, that can ever bring an intense feeling, even to those who focus on them the most. Nobody can be delighted at the idea that they have two arms: but, by reflecting often on the great number of evils that might happen to us, we more easily forgive those that do come. Our condition is better when we submit to it gracefully, than when we uselessly revolt against it.

We ordinarily regard the blessings given by nature and fortune as debts they're repaying us, and consequently we accept them with a kind of indifference; misfortune, on the other hand, seems like injustice, and we receive it impatiently and bitterly. Such false ideas must be rectified. Misfortune is very common, and is our natural due: blessings are quite rare, and these are flattering exceptions made in our favor to the general rule.

Happiness is, in effect, far rarer than we might think. I consider happy he who possesses a certain thing that I want, and which I think would make me happy: its possessor is unhappy; my condition is spoiled by my deprivation of what he has, his is spoiled by other deprivations. Everyone shines with a false luster in the eyes of others, everyone is envied while they themselves are envious; and if being happy were a vice or an absurdity, people would send it back to each other no faster than they do. Those most accused of it, the powerful, rulers, kings, would precisely be the least guilty of all. Let's shed this illusion that shows us far more happy people than there truly are; and we would either be flattered to be in their number, or less irritated not to be so.

Since goods are so scarce, we must not neglect any of those that fall to our lot; however, they are used as in a time of abundance, and as if we had as much as we wanted: we don't think to stop and enjoy those we possess; often we abandon them to chase after those we don't have. We hold the present in our hands; but the future is a kind of charlatan, who, by dazzling our eyes, makes it vanish. Why do we let it toy with us? Why do we allow vain and doubtful hopes to steal certain enjoyments from us? It is true that for many, these hopes are enjoyable in themselves, and can only enjoy what they don't have. Let's leave them with this kind of possession which is so imperfect, so intranquil, so agitated, since they can have nothing else; it would be too cruel to take it from them: but let us try, if possible, to bring ourselves back to the present, to what we have; no blessing should lose all its value only because it has been granted to us.

We usually feel contempt about the minor blessings, but we don't feel the same for the second-rate evils. These things should at least be equal. If our appreciation of the minor blessings is overshadowed by the idea of the greater things we aspire to, the idea of the great misfortunes we might have endured should console us for the minor ones.

As for the minor blessings that we neglect, what do we know if they aren't the only ones we'll ever receive? They are gifts from a greedy power, which way well decide to give us nothing else. Very few men haven't sometimes felt regret for some state, some situation, the happiness of which they failed to appreciate at the time. Very few haven't found some of their complaints against fate to be unwise. Ingratitude has been shown, and punishment has been given.

We should not, say the strict philosophers, place our happiness in everything that doesn't depend on us; this would be risking too much. Such a magnificent principle must be trimmed down: but the more that can be preserved, the better. Let us imagine that our happiness must depend on us completely, and that it's usurpation for external things to wield so much control: let's reclaim such an important right, so dangerous to entrust to others, as much as we can; let's restore to our power that which was detached from it unjustly.

From the start, we must question, so to speak, the authority of anything which would claim to give orders about our happiness; few things will withstand this examination, if this is rigorous at all. Why is this title I'm chasing so necessary? It's because we want to be higher than others. And why so? To receive their respect and praise. And what will this homage and respect do for me? It will tickle me very much. And how will this tickle me, if it's only paid to my title, and not myself personally? The same applies to many other ideas which have taken a very important place in my mind: if I besieged them, they couldn't hold out for long. Yes, some would offer more resistance than others: but as they are more uncomfortable and dangerous, we must return to the charge more often and more courageously. There is no fancy that can be gradually undermined, and which won't finally fall under the force of reflection.

But since we cannot break with all that surrounds us, which external objects will we grant any power over us? Those from which more is to be hoped than feared. It's only a question of calculation, and wisdom must always keep its chips in hand. What are those pleasures worth, and what are the troubles worth which we expend for their sake, or which would come as a result? To be sure, different minds change values, and one price may be good for one person and bad for another. However, there is nearly a universal price affixed to the central things; and everyone agrees, for example, that love is somewhat costly: but it also refuses to be appraised.

As for the surest way, we must go back to the simple pleasures, such as the tranquility of life, company, hunting, reading, etc. If they were only less costly than the others in proportion as they are less lively, they wouldn't deserve this preference, and the other sort would merit their place as much as these do theirs: but the simple pleasures are still pleasures, and they cost nothing. A further great advantage is the fact that fortune can never take them from us. Although it is not reasonable to attach our happiness to all that is most vulnerable to the caprices of chance, it seems that most often we carefully select the least secure places to place it there. We prefer to have all our wealth on a ship than deep in the earth. Finally, the intense pleasures are only moments, and moments that often become terrible from an excess which leaves no sweet aftertaste; whereas the simple pleasures are usually as long-lasting as you like; and they spoil nothing that follows them.

Those who are accustomed to the violent surges of passion will certainly consider bland all the happiness that might be produced by the simple pleasures. What they call insipid, I call tranquil; and I agree that the life most filled with these sorts of pleasures is nothing but a tranquil life. But what sort of idea must people have of the human condition, that they would complain that their life is only tranquil? And what becomes of the most delightful state imaginable, after the initial flame burns out? It becomes a state of tranquility; which is the best thing that could happen to it.

There is no man who, in the course of his life, hasn't had some happy events, pleasant times or moments. Our imagination detaches them from all that preceded or followed them; it gathers them, and imagines a life composed of nothing but them: and it would label this as happiness; this is what it aspires to, perhaps without daring to confess it to itself. It remains certain that all the languishing intervals which, in even the happiest situations, are very long and numerous, we nearly see these as if they shouldn't exist. But they remain, and they are quite inseparable from them. There is no spirit in chemistry so lively that doesn't also have much phlegm in it; the most delightful state also has much of the same, much time that is dull, which we must try to take in stride.

Often, the happiness we have in mind is too complex and too complicated. How many things, for example, would be necessary for a courtier to be happy? Credit with the ministers, the King's favor, considerable establishments for himself and his children, good luck in the games, faithful mistresses to flatter his vanity; finally, everything that an unbridled and insatiable imagination could think of. This man could only be happy at great cost; certainly nature won't pay the bill.

The happiness we propose for ourselves will always be all the easier to obtain, as fewer different things are involved, and as they are less independent of us. The machine will be simpler, and also more under our control.

If we are almost well-off, we should believe we're completely well-off. Often, we will ruin everything to capture this blessing entirely. Nothing is as delicate or fragile as a happy state; we must fear to touch it, even on the pretext of amelioration.

Most of the ways a man improves his state, better the place he holds in society, his volume, so to speak: but this greater volume offers a larger target for the blows of fortune. Would a soldier in the trenches want to become a giant, only to receive more bullets? He who wants to be happy reduces and narrows himself as far as possible. He has these two characteristics; he moves little, and doesn't cling to it.

The greatest secret for happiness is to be on good terms with oneself. Naturally all the troubling accidents that come from without, throw us back at ourselves, and it is good to have a pleasant place to retreat to; but it can never be this way if it hasn't been prepared by the hands of virtue. None of the indulgence of self-love keeps anyone from criticizing themselves for at least a part of what we should indeed criticize: and how disturbed are we by the humiliating concern of hiding from others, for fear of being known, and the inevitable sorrow this would bring? We fly from it, and rightly so: only the virtuous person can see and recognize themselves. I'm not saying that he meditates for the sake of admiring and applauding himself: and could he even do so, as virtuous as he might be? But, since we always love ourselves plenty, we only need to be able to meditate without shame in order to meditate with pleasure.

It may well happen that virtue leads neither to riches nor status, and that on the contrary it excludes such things: one's enemies have great advantages over it with respect to the acquisition of these sorts of goods. It might also happen that glory, its most natural reward, fails to come: it might even deprive itself thereof; at least, by not seeking it out, there will be a risk of losing it. But an unfailing reward is our inner satisfaction. Each duty we fulfill is repaid at the same moment: we can, without pride, appeal to ourselves for the injustice of fate; we find consolation for it by the legitimate testimony that we didn't deserve it; we find in our own reason and in our uprightness a greater source of happiness than others expect from the caprice of chance.

A wish remains to be made about something we're not in control of, for we have only spoken of those which were within our dispositions; this is being placed by fate in a mediocre condition. Without that, both happiness and virtue would be at too great a risk. This is the mediocrity that is so highly recommended by the philosophers, so highly praised by the poets, and sometimes so neglected by all of them.

I agree that this happiness lacks something which, according to common ways of thinking, would still be quite necessary; it has no luster. The happy person we're assuming wouldn't pass for one; he wouldn't have the pleasure of being envied: in addition, maybe he himself will have trouble believing himself happy, for lack of being thought so by others; for, their jealousy helps ensure us of our state, so uncertain are our ideas about everything, which require support. But ultimately, for what little this happy person compares themselves to those whom the vulgar think are happier than him, he readily feels the advantages of his situation; he will gladly resolve himself to enjoy a modest and unknown happiness, the display of which will insult nobody: one's pleasures, like those of discreet lovers, will be seasoned with mystery.

After all that, this wise man, this virtuous man, this happy man remains a man; he has not attained some unshakeable state which the human condition doesn't offer; he might lose everything, even as his own fault. He will preserve his wisdom or his virtue all the better, as he is less proud of it; and his happiness, as he ensures it less.

A DISCOURSE ON PATIENCE

Which won the Prix d'Eloquence by the judgment of the Academie Francaise, in the year 1689.

Whatever employment Men make of their intellect in self-examination, they will discover an abundance of weakness and disorder; reason immediately seeks to apply a remedy, naturally touched by a wish for perfection, a vestige of the ancient greatness to which it was once raised. But what can it now do, uncertain, blind, error-prone, numbered among Man's miseries? It can only fight defects with other defects, or heal passions with other passions; and the vain remedies it provides are evils all the greater and incurable as it has an interest in ceasing to call them evils, and as it is seduced by them.

In vain during many Centuries did Greece, so fertile in subtle, curious and anxious thinkers, produce these Sages who made a brazen profession of teaching their Disciples the arts of living happy, and making themselves more perfect; in vain the infinite diversity of their opinions, which will forever be the shame of the weakness of the natural intellect, exhausted everything that human reason could do for men; the result of the best efforts of Philosophy was only to change the vices produced by corrupt nature into false virtues, which were, if possible, even surer signs of corruption. A common man is either ignorant or he recognizes his defects with great frankness, make them somehow excusable; whereas a Pagan Philosopher, proud of having acquired his by dint of meditation and study, gave his applause to all of them.

These disorders which human reason caused in Greece, where it reigned with all the arrogance it is capable of when it's mistaken, the deceptive Lessons it posted from there to all the Peoples of the world who received them too passively, were surely not the least motives which beckoned the eternal Reason to descend to Earth. If, on one side with the Jews, the famous Weeks of Daniel which had expired, and the Scepter of Judah which had passed into foreign hands, urged the so long promised and awaited Liberator onward, it is certain that, on another hand, the Greeks, delivered so long to prideful errors, and to a self-contented ignorance, equally implored the Messiah by their needs, although they had no right to expect one. God owed it to some to detach his word, so often given by the mouth of his Prophets; and he owed it to others to satisfy his goodness, which couldn't allow them to go on erring in their own wisdom. Some required a Monarch who set up a divine Empire over the Nations, a High Priest to teach them the true Sacrifices; and others needed a Sage to give them sound precepts, a Teacher to bring them all the knowledge for which they had sighed for so long.

There appeared, therefore, among Men, this Messiah so ardently desired by a single People, and so necessary for all of them. Then the ideas of both truth and goodness were revealed to us without obscurity and without fogs; then vanished all these phantoms of virtues which had been begotten by the imaginations of the Philosophers; then the wholly divine remedies were applied effectively to all the ills that are natural to us.

Let us pause, in particular, on one of the effects produced by the new Law proclaimed by JESUS CHRIST. Impatience in evils is perhaps one of the vices to which we're led by nature, most generally and powerfully so; and there is no virtue to which Philosophy has aspired more than patience, no doubt because none is more necessary for the miserable condition of Man, or more capable of gaining a glorious distinction for those who might acquire it. This impatience of Nature, and the false patience of Philosophy, will serve as examples of the happy renewal which then came to the Universe. Let's see how the true patience, heretofore unknown on Earth, took the place of both of these. Let's not be ashamed to look up close and study our miseries from this perspective, such an examination will better convince us of the benefits of our Redeemer.

FIRST POINT.

What is this impetuous movement of our soul which is irritated by the ills we suffer, and which twists and turns to shake off this yoke? Why try to drive them away with violent efforts, which are evidently powerless for this? Why single out, either the Stars which have in no way contributed to our misfortune, or Fortune and Destinies which have no Existence outside of our imagination? What do these complaints mean, addressed to a thousand objects which cannot hear them? What is the meaning of this rage against ourselves, which is even less well founded than any other sort of fit? Do we want comfort in our pains, or to double their number? How wretched we are if we have only such mad and irrational remedies! How insane to double them! But is there any doubt on this point? It is only too obvious that we double our evils. This effort we make to tear out the bolt that wounded us, only lodges it deeper: the soul tears itself by this new agitation; and its unusual motions excite its sensibility, give greater purchase to the pain which torments it.

However, neither the shame of following disordered movements, nor the fear of increasing our suffering, can repress our impatience. People give in all the more easily, since the secret voice of our conscience hardly criticizes us for this, and since these flights of ours seem to have nothing undue or horrid about them. On the contrary, it seems that our suffering is sufficient justification; it seems to dispense us for a certain time from the necessity of being reasonable. Don't we even use a kind of art to excuse ourselves for this defect, and to indulge it without scruple? Don't we often disguise impatience under the sweeter name of vivacity? It is true that it always reveals a soul that has been defeated, and forced to submit; but there are misfortunes in which Men approve of excessive sensibility, and events where they imagine that it's fine to lack forces, and forget oneself completely. Then one is allowed to go as far as respecting impatience, if not applauding it. Who would believe that something that betrays a lack of courage could ever be a basis for vanity? Only religion can remedy a defect so deeply rooted in Nature, and sometimes authorized by our false opinions. It teaches us to suppress in us the impatience that is always harmful and insane, that we are all sinners; that we owe an atonement to the Divine Justice; that we deserve any evil we might suffer. What a strange consolation, judging it from the first ideas that offer themselves! But, wait: we would not only be miserable, we would also have to feel guilty about it? Will we lose even the right to bemoan our fate? Will even the innocence of our sighs be taken from us? Once more, what an odd sort of consolation!

And yet it is one, and it's both solid and effective. As sad as the Heavenly truths sometimes seem, they only come for our happiness and peace. A Christian who is fully persuaded that he deserves what he gets is far from doubling his suffering with his impatience. It is right for the revolt of our soul against the pains due to our sins to be punished by the increase of these same pains; but they can be spared by submitting without complaint to the punishment we receive. It isn't that Christians want suffer less; it's that virtuous acts normally have natural and inseparable rewards. Nobody can have a holy disposition to suffer, unless the harshness of the suffering is diminished. Nobody can consent to suffering without some comfort, and when we choose, contrary to our wishes, the side of divine Justice, it might be said that we weaken, in a way, the power it would have against us.

Must I also class among the motives of patience taught by Religion, the eternal blessings it teaches us to merit by the proper usage of our evils? Are they truly evils, these means of acquiring these celestial blessings which can never be taken from us? Does suffering continue when a man has these in view? And does the idea thereof leave in our soul any room for ephemeral pains and weaknesses? Oh! It seems that they keep us from feeling them, more than they help us endure them.

This was the art of God's kindness; that, even amid the punishments which his wrath sends to us, it has found a way to provide us with a source of infinite happiness. Let us receive such just punishments with sincere submission, and they will immediately become meritorious. Not only will be have effaced our crimes, we will have acquired a right to the supreme Felicity. Blindness of nature, celestial Lights of Religion, how contrary the two of you are! Nature, by her disordered movements, increases our pains, and Religion turns them, so to speak, to profit by the patience it inspires in us. If we heed the former, we add to the necessary evils a voluntary evil; and if we follow the instructions of the latter, we take from these necessary evils the greatest of all boons.

Thus, Christian patience is not a simple patience; it's a true love of pain. Without the sight of this eternity of happiness, the enjoyment of which it assures us, we might limit ourselves to accepting them without complaint, as due punishment for our sins; but in consideration of the infinite reward that will compensate for them, we can only joyfully accept them as favors we don't deserve. This is what produced these miracles which fill up the Christian Chronicles; this tranquility of the Saints even amid the bitterest torments; this perfect equality they have always found between goods and evils: or rather, this preference they have always given to evil over good; these happy excesses of patience they have pushed as far as venturing to call upon themselves certain evils which the hand of God refused them.

What sort of a spectacle, for the corrupt world, was the birth of Christianity! They saw the sudden appearance and universal spread of Men who disagreed with all others on the most common principles; Men who rejected all that is most ardently sought after, with a sincere love for what everyone else flees. Complaint is a language unknown to them, save perhaps amid prosperity. They are not content with an unshakable constancy amid their evils, they possess a joy which often runs to ecstasy; if they don't volunteer for torture and death, they compel themselves to it; the cruelty of their enemies is eternally mistaken; they are only tormented as much as they want to be. What manner of miracles are these? the Pagans must have asked. What kind of revolution is this? Have good and evil traded their natures? Have Men changed this themselves? This astonishment was surely all the greater as Philosophers were seen who, thus far, had seemed to be in possession of all the virtues and truths, confounded both in their speculation and in their practice by new, incomparably more perfect Philosophers. It was these last Sages, or rather it was their celestial Master who destroyed the false patience established by the deceptive Sages, which was perhaps more defective than the impatience that comes naturally to Men who have only the passions for their guides.

SECOND POINT.

Never has human reason shown itself so prideful, and put on display so much powerlessness, as in the Sect of the Stoics. These Philosophers undertook to convince Mankind that their own body was something foreign to them, the interests of which should be indifferent to them, and that the pains which afflicted this body were ignored by the Sage, which were completely distinct from the spiritual part of himself. Thus, the Stoic regarded evils with contempt, as enemies incapable of doing him harm; and he assumed a pompous patience, based on the impassiveness on which his Sect flattered itself. To suffer with constancy would have been too human, he didn't suffer at all, like Jupiter himself, in whose perfections and happiness he took no interest.

How far will you err, weak human minds, when you are left to yourselves? Indeed! To soothe the wounds we receive, we moan about them, and no other remedy is concocted but to claim invulnerability? We would be only too lucky if we could enter into this illusion and gain any benefit; but, if these vain ideas rise for a few moments and inflate the seduced imagination, we are immediately recalled to the pain of our evils by the strongest and most powerful nature; and if that sectarian stubbornness which has been chosen, still maintains this arrogant speculation in the mind, the heart's suffering belies and condemns it. When this Stoic, pressed by the pain of a violent malady, cried when addressing it: *I still refuse to confess that you are an evil*; this effort of his in refusing, this even apparent disavowal, was clearly a confession of the strongest and most sincere sort!

Far from Christianity be an error so contrary to the natural feelings, and the sort of pride which is so unworthy of an enlightened reason. The patience of Christians is not based on what they imagine to be above pain; they suffer, they admit that they suffer; but their submission for he who makes them rightly suffer, but the prize which is held up in return for their sufferings, produces this constancy, this calm, this joy which so often forces their Persecutors to respect and admire them. They don't restrain their complaints and moans from any fear of dishonoring the party they profess to follow; but the divine Religion they follow suppresses in them all complaints and moans by the holy thoughts it gives them. They are internally the way the Stoics took great pains to appear externally: the calm victors of the pain they endure. They are precisely that which all of Philosophy couldn't admire too highly, as sensible as all other Men are to all human suffering, more satisfied amid the greatest miseries, than if they were the most fortunate of Men.

Nowhere does patience shine to greater advantage than amid insults. A Stoic who was offended only kept a peaceful exterior, because he immediately rose, in his heart, above the perpetrator, and sometimes even by an arrogant Judgment dared to debase him below the human level; which is an insult without danger from one's enemy, an impotent vengeance which additionally consoles one's pride. A Christian puts his heart below all Men, and yet he possesses, through all insults, a heroic tranquility which places him above his enemies. What an innocent and happy artifice does grace teach us! Without assuming a baseless pride, without affecting a false insensibility, we have only to humble ourselves under the Creator's hand to be superior to all Creatures: we have only to respect this in the instruments it employs, to suffer the harshest blows Men can deal us. None aren't powerful enough to make us suffer; but also, none are powerful enough to upset our repose. When their arms are turned against us, a more powerful arm, which drives their action, reveals itself to the eyes of our faith, keeps our pain respectful, and represses all the agitation they might produce in our soul. The injustice we have to suffer is no longer represented to us as events caused by Human wickedness, which excites our hatred and indignation; we rise higher, and with a clearer sight we discover that the same events come from Heaven, and as due punishments which require submission, and as sources of merit which call for gratitude.

Things were different when judging most of the Philosophers, who were convinced that all things were governed by a blind, immutable, necessary fatality, from which all good and evil came without distinction. It is true that they submitted to it in their misfortune, and sometimes with much resolve; but what was this kind of patience? A patience of Slaves attached to their chain, and subject to all the whims of a ruthless Master; a patience which, based as it was only on the futility of revolt, harshly arrests the movements of the soul, and instead of consolation, leaves it with a somber and bewildered sorrow; in a word, a thoughtful despair, rather than a true patience. Thanks to our august Religion, we know that we don't depend on a blind destiny, which invincibly carries us and drags us along. Our misfortunes don't come from the fortuitous arrangement of what surrounds us; an eternal Intelligence that is no less powerful than their imaginary fatality seemed to the Philosophers, but also a supremely wise one, presides over all things. This arm whose blows we feel, is an arm which distributes us misfortune according to our needs and our forces, which, properly speaking, only sends us blessings, it's the arm of a father; we suffer like children, sure of the goodness inherent in he who causes our suffering, and not like Slaves subjected to all the bizarre and cruel forms of harshness; it's not the futility of the revolt that stops us, but the injustice of rebellion, and our patience is a true submissiveness of the mind which spreads in the heart a consolation nearly as sweet, I dare say, as the enjoyment of any blessing.

These are the effects produced among Christians by the Divine example of patience which was held up for them, when the Just, the only just man who was ever just by himself, found himself on the point of atoning for the sins of Humanity. Abandoned by all of Nature, aside from a few Disciples, who gave him no more than a few moments of faithfulness, awed by the fearsome sight of an execution equally ignominious and cruel that was his destiny, he addresses his celestial Father, asking him to spare him if possible the torments he envisages: and a wish that the magnitude of his already manifest torments rendered so legitimate, a wish even more legitimate by the innocence of he who made it, a wish where moderation shines forth even in the terms which express it, is however repressed in the same moment, by an entire and unreserved submissiveness to the designs of God. *May thy will be done*, said JESUS CHRIST to his Father; and what was this will! How severe and rigorous he knew it to be in his case! He saw himself handed over to wrathful Justice, he saw kindness entirely suspended; however, to satisfy the duties of filial obedience, he subscribes to his own disgrace, and his only comfort amid his intensest pains is to turn his eyes to the hand from which he received them.

He again sighed on the Cross, he complained of having been abandoned by his Father; but he did not murmur about this extreme strictness; he only showed us how strongly it affected him. The Philosophers claimed impassivity, which in the state we're in cannot agree with human nature, and JESUS CHRIST refused to enjoy that which he could have received from his Divinity. He suffered the cruelest torments to leave an example suitable to Men, who are necessarily subject to pain. He took all our sensibility to lead us with greater force to the imitation of his patience.

Inspire in us, O Word incarnate, this heroic virtue so far from the corruption which has become natural to us, and from the false perfection to which Philosophy aspired. Condescend to instruct us in the science of suffering; a wholly celestial science, and which belongs only to your Disciples. The whole course of your Life gives us amazing Lessons of this; but how can we put them into practice without the help of your grace? From you alone can we gain a true idea of the virtues, and only you, too, can give us the power to follow them. You, who are the Reason and Wisdom of your adorable Father, thus become ours, to regulate the excesses to which nature is abandoned in affliction. Do not allow, Lord, your Justice to bring them upon us, until you have given to our soul the dispositions necessary to profit from them; and don't send us all the evils we deserve, unless you also give us a truly Christian courage.

THE STORY OF THE AJAOIANS

OR

The relation of a voyage by Mr. S. VAN DOELVELT to the Orient, in 1674, which contains the description of the Government, of the Religion and of the Morals of the Nation of the Ajaoians. Translated from the original Flemish.

NOTICE

Which must be read.

Indeed, People tend to pass over these beginnings of books, and rightly so, since so often these notes, prefaces and notices are only a jumble of words in praise of the author's work. The present one isn't of this sort; here neither the author, who is presently buried more than 1600 leagues away, nor his Memoirs, which everyone can judge as they will, or even the translation which has no other quality than its accuracy. What, then, is the purpose of this notice? It's to keep the reader from forming a rash judgment of Mr. van Doelvelt. These Memoirs are written in a way that takes sides and supports the cause of the Ajaoians. Which might lead the reader, who can only be informed by the last Chapter of these Memoirs, why he acts as he does; it might, I repeat, lead one to accuse this good man of betraying Religion and sacrificing it in favor of a people with none at all. This relation must, therefore, be read as the work of the Ajaoians themselves; for, as will be seen in this final Chapter, Mr. van Doelvelt, accepted as a citizen of Ajao, has embraced all the opinions in such a sincere manner that, having returned to Europe, he worked with all his heart to make converts; and he only returned to Ajao because he saw that it would be impossible for him to make his compatriots, or at least his best friends, Ajaoians. I have thought it best to warn the reader of these circumstances, both for the sake of the author's honor, and for the reader's satisfaction: I will inform him that Mr. van Doelvelt returned to Ajao, to his wives and his children, in 1682. Since, while departing, he made a promise to his friends that he would send word of the success of his voyage, some letters did, indeed, arrive from him, signed from Laontung in Tartary, on the border of China, where he arrived in good health, and from whence he hoped to go and see his dear homeland again, and breathe the healthy and pure air of Ajao, within two months. This leads us to expect that he arrived in good health.

FIRST CHAPTER: A SHORT ACCOUNT OF THE VOYAGE OF MR. S. VAN DOELVELT. ON HIS ARRIVAL AMONG THE AJAOIANS, AND HOW HE WAS RECEIVED BY THEM.

Oppressed by the troubles that were tearing my country apart, and which were caused by those factious spirits who, in all parties, were driven by wholly shameful motives of self-seeking, hatred and ambition, I formed a resolution to travel abroad, hoping that, at my return, I would find the factions which I couldn't support dissipated, without incurring any guilt, either of injustice before the tribunal of my conscience, or treason against my country.

A cousin I had in Zealand, who was highly credited due to his great wealth and his position as a *Bewindhebber*[24] of the East India Company, supplied me the means of executing my project, by finding me an important place on one of the ships departing at the end of 1673.

Since my only plan is to share the history of the happy nation of the Ajaoians, I will pass silently over all that my

---

[24] An Associate or Director. (Translator note: These footnotes are from the original text.)

journal contains about what happened along the journey, and what I've thought worthy of sharing; many others have spoken, before my departure and after my return, of such things.

Having arrived at Batavia, I presented my letters of recommendation to the General and the Director-General, who offered me all their services, so that, in consideration of my cousin, I found myself in the other world, so to speak: in a position to amply satiate my thirst for discovery, which I had always possessed, fully resolved to eternalize my name, baptizing as *Doelvetsland* the first uninhabited or unknown shore I found. But it wasn't one of these passing and imperfect discoveries that I needed. I wanted, at the cost of all my blood, to discover, as a competent man, and not like those numb-skulls and lazy-asses who, content merely to wave at the coasts they discover, hardly put their feet on the ground to examine the nature of the land.

My resolution didn't displease the Directors, who were eager for such discoveries, which can only contribute to the propagation of their empire into that country. Thus, I was allowed to carry out all the plans for discovery that I thought reasonable, and four pilots were put under my command, who were among the best at navigating the seas of unknown lands.

Around the middle of the year 1675, after many useless expeditions toward the southern lands, an occasion arose that was too favorable not to be seized. It was a case of discovery, which says it all. The rumor that had spread was that some Moscovite rafts, or from the White Sea, after having been cast in every direction by fearful storms, had washed up on the coasts of Niphom, had given the idea to a few members of the Regency to discover a new route, to cross from the Indies to Holland, going north of Tartary and of all of Scandinavia. I was consulted about such a fine plan; I didn't fail to give it my praise, and I even offered to join the team.

Everything was soon ready for our new expedition; and with the representations given to His Japanese Majesty, of the great advantages that his subjects would derive from such a discovery, he assured us that in case any storm drove us into his lands, or if we should run short of supplies on this unknown route, we would be permitted to recuperate on the coast of Nanhu[25].

The four ships which were to have the glory of this discovery were loaded with all the necessities. Neither offensive nor defensive weapons were neglected, nor were the instruments to protect our ships against the northern ice, and we took as we left a half-dozen flat constructions to help with our descent. I can't help but point out that these were my own invention, and describe them here.

It was one of these barges used in the Indies to carry merchandise from one Island to another, but I had reinforced them. Reinforcing barges! How pitiful! Pity as much as you like, that's just what I did, here's how. Since

---

[25] Northeast of the Island of Niphom.

these boats were only made for descents, it occurred to me that if they were boarded on the side, we would have the entire length of the flank, on which the soldiers, standing side by side, could fire more extensively, more easily, and, filling more space, could repel more of those who dared to oppose our descent. To facilitate these boardings from the side, I ordered the construction, with strong poles and tarred twine, of a kind of artificial beak, which was put in the water against the side of the ship, by means of the pulleys that I had placed towards the poop. This beak had the same effect on the ship's side as these angles that are made opposite those flying buttresses on bridges, breaking the water's current; and two rudders, which I had set opposite the pulleys, served to guide the barge against the coasts, towards which it could easily advance in this situation, since this artificial beak cut the water which otherwise would have battered the flank too powerfully. Having found this way of landing, I looked for a way to cover the soldier, and discovered nothing better than to have a kind of parapet constructed, on the right side of the boat; and to keep my bark balanced, I had as much ballast put on the left side as wood was used in this parapet, which covered the soldier up to his head, by means of a kind of half-arch that I had made on its crest. This sheltered him from attack, if we had to descend on a steep slope where the locals would be higher than the boat and its parapet. This is about the full description of my fortified boat, which was very useful in what follows, but not against the Ajaoians, as will soon be seen.

Departing from the port of Batavia, we carried, as we passed, the orders from the General to several Islands that were on our way: and, since we had chosen the season when the southern winds are nearly always predominant in these seas, we soon passed by all the Islands of Japan; and having passed the strait of the Ories we ran eastward, to try to rediscover the lands that had already been discovered by certain Japanese pilots.

We hadn't sailed a hundred leagues to the northeast before we came across something. We immediately opened all our sails toward this thing, but the next morning, just when we thought we were very close to it, it immediately vanished: which led us to believe that it was some fearsome whale that had spent the night there. But its flight gave us a more real joy, for we discovered, behind the space it had occupied, something that we judged certainly to be land. Indeed, we could make out peaks and valleys; our spy-glasses even showed us vegetation. Thus, we continued on our way. We then found ourselves around 48 degrees 12 min. of latitude and around 197 of longitude. The night which then overtook us was accompanied by a great calm, which pleased us greatly, afraid as we had been of crashing, whether against these unknown shores, or against some reef.

Once the dawn gave us a view of where we were and where we had traveled, we took measures to assure ourselves whether it really was land; and after much speculation, u-turns and some tacking, we were convinced that it was indeed, and even that it had to be a large Island.

Certain on this point, we held a small council on the best way to make our descent, and after hearing and examining many ideas, we agreed that we should approach by night with our four ships, keeping a reasonable distance from the land, so that they would be accessible to our fortified barges, which would advance to the shores at dawn, with most of our men, to make the descent, without being seen, if possible.

The constant and impertinent prejudice of ours, that peoples not of our own continent are so many brutish barbarians, then made us suppose that these strangers, if there were any, wouldn't be clever enough to have sentinels on their borders, as we have in our Europe; but we were gravely mistaken: for, as I'll explain, we were discovered, probably before we discovered them; and we were defensively awaited, before we had held our war-council.

But, *quanta cadunt inter humana supremaque labra!* Our plan was nearly executed when, around the third hour of night there arose such a terrible storm that it was impossible to keep our ships close together. Our four ships initially sailed off, while our barges became the playthings of the winds and waves, and, as I later learned, after returning to Batavia, only three rejoined the four ships, more than ten days after this storm, with great difficulty and after much fear.

As for the one I happened to be in, along with 160 men, it was cast on the sands of this unknown land, where we crashed, after being exposed for 24 hours to the winds, and we were nearly submerged a hundred times.

We weren't there for long and we were given no time to deliberate or take any precautions. The fatigue and terror that my soldiers had suffered had them so shattered that they were incapable of self-defense, if the peoples of this land had been as barbaric as we had imagined. But, how astonished we were when, at the moment we least expected, we saw them running in a mass towards the debris of our bark, to be ruthlessly massacred, we saw them lay their weapons down in unison, and invite us with their gestures to follow them and have no fear.

We wanted to confer on what to do, and we cast our eyes all around to see if we might find any way out. But all we could see was the furious waves: so, we assembled for deliberation. Then, one of the most visible members of the troop approached us, along with another one who seemed to be under his orders. They seemed to have come closer only to examine our manners, and so everyone spoke freely, convinced that these strangers didn't understand us. But we were soon disabused, for, after one of our officers suggested we follow these strangers, but to be on guard, hiding our pistols and bayonets under our cloaks, so that they could only take our lives at great cost, if they meant any violence; the one who accompanied this leader of the inhabitants told him a few words in the local language, after which, addressing me and giving me his hand, said:

"Good Dutch Christians", he said in good Dutch[26], "you aren't dealing here with scoundrels like Spaniards or the Portuguese, and so your precautions are useless; we know what your pistols and rifles can do, and we won't allow them into our city. Leave them here on the shore with some of your men to guard them, until you receive the orders of our Supreme Magistrate."

You can imagine how shocked we were to hear our own language from one of these barbarians. There was no longer any question of deliberation; I only wanted to excuse the suspicious thoughts of my comrade, and to beg this interpreter to interpose his services for us wretches whom the winds and tempest had cast upon unknown lands; that Providence had placed us in their hands and that they could do with us as they pleased, since they were aware that a hundred poor fellows could never resist an entire people. He cut me off, assuring me that we had nothing to fear, if we subjected ourselves to the just orders that the Supreme Magistrate would give us, without however assuming that we would submit against our will; that I would be led before this Supreme Magistrate, since I was the Chief of this unfortunate troop; that I would be treated with all possible kindness; and that after having interrogated me, the Supreme Magistrate would gave me his orders personally.

---

[26] It will be seen, Chap. VII, how these peoples gained knowledge of the morals and languages of foreign nations.

I asked him how I should behave in this audience. "You men," he told me, "only need to follow this troop which is marching leftward; as for you, you will be given a horse, and you will go with four of our principal Officers by another path, by which you will arrive at the city at the same time as your men, who will be lodged in a large house outside the city, where the four Officers will lead to you fetch clothes similar to ours. After which they will lead you before the Supreme Magistrate, to whom they will give a report of your misadventure. I will appear there to serve as your spokesman: there you can speak with the same confidence as with a group of your best friends; for, without knowing you, that's exactly what we all are, and there is nobody here who wouldn't shed his blood for you, and for each member of your troop."

This humanity delighted me, I regretted parting ways with my affable interpreter who would accompany our people, and I followed the officer who was with him, and when three others joined him I was given a horse, and we started on the road to the city.

Since I intend to give a description of this country, I will only mention in passing that I have never seen anything as beautiful as the landscape we crossed. Abundance was everywhere on display, its order and symmetry were amazing, its meadows were covered with livestock: cows, steer, horses, sheep, goats, everything was there in flocks, of extraordinary size in comparison with our own. The trees were bowed under the weight of all manner of fruit. In a word, nothing was more pleasant than the sight of the riches of this fertile land.

I found myself within sight of a large city, without realizing how far we had traveled.

I also saw my men marching on the other side, and we converged on a large house called the *Foreigner's Guesthouse*, of which we were put in charge by lodging us there. A man, who I took for a slave, came to present me with a greenish material, which was neither serge nor woollen cloth, and which might be compared with our *pinchinas*. Since it was only a kind of dressing-gown or long coat with sleeves, I soon had it on my shoulders, and in this get-up I followed my four guides or guards, who led me in the city of Ajao, which I will describe elsewhere.

We crossed many streets that looked very alike, until, coming to a large plaza, we found ourselves face to face with a huge palace to which I soon realized that I was being led, and imagining that this might be the dwelling of the Sovereign, I adjusted my new clothing the way I saw my guides wearing theirs (for everyone is dressed the same way in this country), and I entered a vast court where I found my interpreter, with whom my guides placed me; after which they vanished up a magnificent staircase. A quarter of an hour later, two men came looking for us, and we climbed this fine staircase, then entered a vast hall, from which we passed to a smaller one, where we saw the Supreme Magistrate, who I will describe.

Twenty-four men around 50 to 60 years of age, seated in a circle on a large carpet, without distinction, either as to rank or in their dress, formed this Supreme Council, which governs with unrivaled wisdom all the affairs of this rather extensive State. The chamber was neither magnificently furnished with marble, nor enriched with sculptures of gold, marble, or azure; the walls, along with the ceiling, coated with a certain locally-made shiny plaster, were of a whiteness that was cleaner than all the ornaments of art. There was neither secretary nor clerk to sell the dispatches of this Supreme Court. Four large books which were in the midst of the circle, one of which was the Register of the Police, the second that of the Judgments and Resolutions, the third that of the Finances, and the fourth that of War and Slaves, contained all the laws of the State, and all the secrets of this wise Magistracy, which I will discuss in another place.

When I was introduced along with my interpreter, we remained standing near the circle, and immediately those Magistrates whose backs or sides had been turned to us, all turned to face us, and the one closest to me addressed me, saying in his language, as my spokesman interpreted, "Foreigner, our people participates in your misfortune, and we are sensibly touched by your shipwreck, all the more as, trading with none of the peoples that surround us, we cannot find a way to send you back to your country. If you are given the means to mend your raft, you might be mad enough to risk perishing in the vast sea, in an effort to depart with great uncertainty in search of your land. But, in good conscience, we cannot occasion the loss of so many men who are useful to Nature. Thus, we find it suitable to burn all that the storm has cast along with you onto our shores; for you to be given a house where your men are already lodged, and for you to stay for fourteen moons to learn the ways of our people. You will be fed and kept in all ways, like any other citizen; and after the expiration of this period, those among you who would rather not live with us, can eventually return to their country. Is this offer agreeable to you? Reply, wise foreigner".

I gave thanks to the Magistrate, and I asked leave to share this offer with my fellows in fortune, on whose behalf I couldn't respond. My request was granted, and I withdrew as I had entered, that is, without ceremony.

I found all my men as impatient as they were anxious; but when they heard my report of the Magistrate's speech, they blessed the moment they had wrecked into a land where they found the means to live in peace and at their ease the rest of their days. It is true that some of them immediately asked if, by consenting to remain, they would be condemned to an eternal celibacy. But I deferred their impatient question to the future, and I returned to the Palace, where I was immediately introduced by my interpreter: I assured the Supreme Magistrate of my men's intention to submit to his just laws, and I asked for someone to be named to confer with me, on the means to be used for our establishment. My request was extremely surprising to this venerable assembly, and one of them spoke, saying: "Friend, here, our affairs are handled in public: this is why we are assembled; speak, you will get an answer."

I asked forgiveness for my ignorance of the laws of the land, and I withdrew, begging leave to appear another time, and to have my interpreter by my side to inform me of all I would need, which was immediately granted.

This is how I arrived at Ajao and how I ended up staying there. Let us pass to the history of the people of this Island, the happiest one on our terrestrial globe, thanks both to the wisdom of its laws, and the strictness with which they are practiced.

CHAPTER II: A DESCRIPTION OF THE ISLAND OF THE AJAOIANS.

We had not been mistaken, when, in our discovery of the land of the Ajaoians, we had thought it an Island. It might be considered one of the most spacious ones; for it was very similar to Sicily, both in extent and shape. It's a country of plains, except to the east, where there are a few mountains which have their use, since from their hearts these people take all the metals they use. From these same mountains comes the river of Ajao, which crosses the Island from east to west, where, by going into the sea, if forms one of the two ports of the Island. This river is enlarged by the waters of two other smaller ones, the Peridi, which flows from south to north, and the Lamo which, originating in a small lake to the north, flows southward. These two rivers empty into the Ajao near an Island which forms the stream, and where the fortress of Fu stands: it is situated on the top of a steep rock in the middle of this Island. The Island is surrounded by the waters of these three rivers, which create a rather large lake, from which the name of this fortress is taken.

These three rivers provide nourishment to such a great quantity of fish of all kinds, except pikes and eels, that everything they say about the abundance of lakes and rivers in Ireland is nothing in comparison. This one lake of Fu could feed the whole Island; for you might almost say that this whole body of fish gathers to facilitate the harvest for the inhabitants.

The mountains on the eastern part of the Island contain enough treasures to gratify the greed of the greediest people in our Europe. But most of it remains buried in their heart, where the Ajaoians extract them only needed. Three mountains furthest north contain such a great quantity of iron that, although it is continually extracted, and has been for more than two thousand years since this Island was populated, the mines remain as abundant as if they were newly opened. The southern mountains are full of gold, but there are only two open mines, where everyone goes and takes as they require. Those near the middle provide silver which is of frequent use among this people, since they use it to make all the things we make of earth, brass, and leather. The reason for this is that none of these metals are found on the Island, and since, if they have earth suitable for pottery, they don't know how to work it. They similarly use gold for things we would make from lead, such as the coverings of public buildings; and since they learned the use of gunpowder, which they only use in cannons, for they don't want any other firearms, they make their bullets from it.

The countrysides are fertile in grains of all sorts: they gather wheat, rye, barley, rice, millet, peas, beans so abundantly that they are sometimes forced to leave all the lands of the Island fallow for a whole year, to keep from having to burn the prior years'.

These plains are so well distributed into arable plots and meadows that, if the former produce so abundantly, the latter are also of great advantage, since they feed the oxen used for tilling, the animals used as food, and the horses which, like us, the Ajaoians use to pull carriages. The wool of their sheep, which is unsurpassed by that of Spain and England, clothes the locals. The cows and steers provide them with more leather than they need to cover their carriages, to make sandals, and to fashion the kinds of rafts they use on their rivers. In a word, this Island provides its inhabitants with all they need, to live the sweetest and happiest life imaginable. I won't even mention their forests, which are full of game (which they hardly eat), which is found everywhere in flocks, like sheep in our meadows. Nor will I mention their fruit trees, which give them all manner of fruits, some we know and some we don't, since these things are according to the fertility mentioned above.

It is true that this Island produces no wine, and that its inhabitants are ignorant of the use of all strong drinks. But this same flaw, if it is one, serves to preserve their health; and their way of preparing a kind of rice beer makes up for it very well. I wouldn't want to claim that this Island has never had vines: for the Ajaoians' slaves, who are the Island's aborigines, have some songs in their language which mention wine. It's a sort of tradition for the Legislators of the Ajaoians to have this plant uprooted, knowing how liable man is to misuse its fruit, and to what extremities he runs by the abuse of something so good in itself.

This Island is divided into six districts or territories, and it the same number of cities, which are Ajai, Jaroi, Lamo, Kalure, Operidi, Dorao; each of which has under them a certain number of good, well-populated villages, as I will mention when I come to the Government.

This Island has only two ports: that of Ajao and that of Jaroi, which are the only two spots where this Island can be accessed. For, as if Nature intended to preserve the Ajaoians from outside visitation, and the consequent corruption from the other peoples on the earth, it placed them amid stones and reefs, which surround their Island and seem to defend it on all sides. Therefore, it must be allowed that it's only chance, or rather good luck, which, amid the storm, led our unfortunate barge precisely through the passage of Ajao, without its breaking on the sandy shores on either side.

CHAPTER III: ON THE RELIGION OF THE AJAOIANS.

In all States religion has such a powerful influence on the government, on the laws, on the politics and on morality that it has occurred to me that, before discussing the laws, the government, and the morality of the Ajaoians, I should convey a good idea of their Religion, or rather, of their views on what is commonly called Religion.

But, before going into this detail, I can't help but confess that I'm afraid that, by judging the views of the Ajaoians about our vulgar notions, feelings of indignation will arise against them, instead of admiration, which is my intention. In effect, we normally imagine that ideas should be the same in all men, and that, since we think a certain way about certain things, everyone else should think like us and share our opinions. Whenever the contrary turns out to be the case, a certain consuming zeal animates us, and we ruthlessly condemn these people who have the same right over us as we imagine we have over them exclusively. We don't take the trouble to consider that prejudices are not the same everywhere, and that, consequently, opinions should differ; in this way, there is injustice in condemning others, because they don't think like us. Since I believe that there is nobody of good sense who doesn't agree with this, I will describe, come what may, the views of the Ajaoians.

These peoples don't recognize any founder of their Republic, or of their Religion. Thus, they have no sects or parties among them, whether in Religion or in affairs of State. They have no holy book nor written law: they only have certain principles emanated from the bosom of the soundest reason, and from Nature itself; principles whose proof and certainty are incontestable, and on which they base all their views and all their opinions. This being the case, can these views ever fail to be secure, sound and pure?

1st Principle: *That which is not, cannot give existence to anything.*

2nd Principle: *Treat others as you would like them to treat you.*

Their views on Religion are derived from the first of these principles; and the second regulates all their conduct, as much civil as political.

Everyone of sound mind will realize that the Ajaoians, following these two principles, consider Nature only as their good mother. Eternal in her existence, they say, and supremely perfect in her essence, she granted existence to all creatures, and in her all things take place with the order necessary for the preservation and maintenance of these same creatures. Behold, therefore, their Deity.

More submissive than we are to the clear lights of a sound and unbiased reason, they don't proceed to invent a chimerical epoch for the birth of the first creatures, which are made to emerge (contrary to their first principle) from the empty hands of a Being who is incomprehensible, invisible, unknown, invented at whim; almost the way a con man lifts a cup to reveal a ball, which he'd already shown the crowd to be empty. The Ajaoians, who are more rational than that, regard this Nature as their mother, whom experience has shown to be the mother common to all creatures who, by an amazing kind of circulation, emerge continually from her and then return. It is true that the past eternity of the universe's existence is no better understood by an Ajaoian than by a Christian; but they candidly acknowledge the limitations of human knowledge: how different they are from us, who rack ourselves inventing false reasons, for no reason but to have a response for everything, rightly or wrongly. Thus, when they are asked how there could be no beginning to the existence of Nature, they confess that this eternity of existence is beyond the grasp of the human mind; but they maintain that they have no less of a right to accept it, since they find nothing contradictory in it: whereas, by assuming a point when Nature began to exist, and some other point where it would have began to produce creatures, reason finds itself in a labyrinth of inexplicable objections and contradictions.

Thus, nothing gives them more of a right to jeer at us Europeans than when, arguing with them, I clearly explained our views on the eternal existence of our God. "Who is more ridiculous," said they, "you or us, on this point? You simply assume your God (for it would be impossible for you to demonstrate his existence a priori[27]) , and you suppose him to be an invisible Being which is everywhere, which, from all eternity has only thought of itself, and who, after some ninety thousand moons, made all of Nature: from what? From nothing. This idea and these attributes of your Deity are as grand and pompous, but also as fantastical, as this Deity itself. This invisibility is cleverly devised. For, in his favor, you can make whatever you like of this God; and his omnipotence is marvelous: for with it, what can the Deity not be said to do, in time of need? We shouldn't be surprised if such a God is the agent of all the governmental scheming in your Europe. What can they not do with such a fine tool at their disposal? But after all, what a detour! This Being made all of Nature, Nature made us (for this is truth comes from experience). We take a shorter path and a more rational one, by considering Nature herself as eternal, which we know has existed for so many centuries, with the same order we find there, which our ancestors saw, and which our descendants will see in it."

The Ajaoians, therefore, believe they're well-grounded in reason to put Nature in the place of what we call God. It is at least certain that neither imagination nor prejudice led them to this choice: for, I've seen that these peoples are absolutely free of such things; and they're far different from us in this way: for, it is clear that we most often defend opinions born of prejudice with other

---

[27] I use this term of the School, to avoid a long and muddled periphrase, and because it conveys the Ajaoians' idea.

prejudices; and that stubbornness, so natural to us, makes us seek all the means of supporting *per fas and nefas*, an opinion which we have once accepted.

Indeed, why do we Christians want Nature to have had a beginning, except that we see everything with respect to ourselves, and that, on one hand, the existence of this universe affecting our senses, and on the other, our pride being forced to recognize a point where we began to exist, makes us readily find the same defect in this great totality that we are a part of. The consolation of the miserable is to have others who are like them. Hence, the idea, or rather the opinion of a Being, God, Master and Author of Nature and ourselves, a Being begotten by the imagination, but unknown to reason, and consequently to the Ajaoians.

It is easy to see that this first and principal opinion of the Ajaoians follows from their conviction on the futility of public ceremonies and worship, and of the mortality of what we call the soul. Thus, these peoples have no temples, altars, or priests. Indeed, since they think they were given existence, motion and life by Nature only, what reason would they have to address prayers to her, to make vows, to burn incense, and to butcher victims in her favor? All these ceremonies tend to nourish the superstition of the masses, to lull them to sleep, and bring success to the scheming of political leaders. Nature is not a capricious ruler, they say, who will change the given order for the price of a few quarters of roasted beef or mutton, clouds of smoke made by a few grains of resin, or a prayer pronounced by the mouth of a hypocrite. Her laws are immutable, her revolutions always occur with the same regularity, and nothing can turn her in the slightest from her ordinary course; thus, these prayers, these vows, these sacrifices are completely futile, burdensome only to those who are stupid enough to submit to them, and advantageous only to those who are their ministers.

Let's come to the soul: this is a being that the Ajaoians don't recognize in any way. This may seem ridiculous, without however being so with respect to these people. For we must imagine these Islanders as a Nation which has nothing in common with other men, except their form, and which has none of our ideas, our prejudices, our fancies, our opinions, except for the pure notions of sound reason; but they follow them, while we repress them. However that may be, why have we imagined inside ourselves this being we call the soul? Except to support the idea of our own Divinity, and at the same time our extraction and supposed resemblance with this God. He created us in his image, we say: we suppose him spiritual: our body can't be the copy of this divine original; something else had to be invented, and a second being was placed in man, which is a part of himself, which knows all and which doesn't know itself.

The Ajaoian reasons differently and without supposition, maybe it's because they lack any idea of a spiritual Being: then, who has the right idea? However it may be, if you ask him whether he's no different from the other animals, he would reply: "No doubt, for all creatures are not invested with equal perfections." This is a true axiom based on daily experience, and on the very nature of things, from which the Ajaoians conclude that they are different from lions, just as lions are different from wolves, etc., because not all creatures have the same perfections.

But, ask him about the origin of this reason with which he is endowed, and he will maintain, with good arguments (which I might produce elsewhere) that, although this reason does distinguish us from the other animals, this is only a matter of degrees, since each animal has some portion of it, and since the difference consists only in the fact that the portion we enjoy is the most excellent one, or because we have a greater portion of it, or finally because our organs are constituted for different functions. An Ajaoian proves this from a thousand examples in nature, and from the ways of most animals, in which all that is found in man in this respect is also evident, albeit to a lesser degree. This will no doubt seem strange to many, but the problem is with their prejudices.

From this, the Ajaoians conclude that that which we call soul is nothing other than a part of this subtle and very fine matter which is predominant throughout all of Nature, and which is distributed within all bodies, more or less, according to the nature of their consistency. This matter originates in the Sun, from which it acquires a continual motion, it's the purest fire in all of Nature. It doesn't burn of itself, but by the different movements it communicates to the particles of the other bodies where it is insinuated, it burns and makes its heat felt. The visible fire, they say, has more of this subtle matter than the air, the latter more than water, and earth even less than that does. Among the mixed creatures, plants have more than minerals, and animals even more. Finally, this fire, insinuated in bodies, renders them capable of sensation, and this is what the Europeans call the soul, which is nothing other than the animal spirits which are spread in all parts of bodies. But, it is certain that this soul, of the same nature as the animals, dissipates upon the death of man, like that of the other animals; thus, everything that the Europeans say about the immortality of their soul is only a chimera invented by cunning political leaders, their lawgivers, to keep them in a continual fear of a supposed future; a fear which must make their lives into a tissue of misery and terror, from which nothing will spare them.

There is no public religious worship, nor is there any priesthood. Their heads of household, in private, attend, every evening, to those who depend on them, to the duties of a good citizen, and to that which society demands from its members. These are the preachers of the Ajaoians: this is the subject-matter of their sermons.

Our prejudiced folk will now ask, "How can a Republic of people with such views subsist?" This will be seen in the remainder of this relation: and I even dare advance that their government is more sound, their morals are more pure, and their laws are better observed than in any other country. "What?" It will be cried, "without a Deity, without fear of an eternal future?" Yes, and don't take my word for it: judge it by its fruits; but, I repeat, we shouldn't judge the Ajaoians by ourselves; they don't have our passions, inclinations, or desires; they know neither our lusts, our ambitions, or our greed; they owe this good fortune to their education: let this be judged without the preconceptions of the corruption of nature. Nature is only corrupted for us, since our parents, teachers, examples, all that surrounds us corrupts it; but it is healthy where its laws alone are recognized, and where no bad examples are mixed in with its sound principles.

CHAPTER IV: ON EDUCATION AND YOUTH AMONG THE AJAOIANS.

The Island of Ajao is divided into six districts, as I've already said, or rather, into six cities, each of which forms a separate Republic. Thus, this Republic is composed of six small individual Republics. When you understand the constitution of any, you understand that of the other five. So, I will stick with that of Ajao, the most spacious of the six, and the one I've visited most often, because it is the residence of the residence of the Supreme Magistrate, which is the only thing that distinguishes it from the rest, and because my residence was assigned there.

Ajao is divided into six triangles, which form so many quarters: each quarter contains between six and eight hundred houses. Each house typically holds twenty families. These are long buildings, separate from each other, like so many small palaces; they are inhabited on the bottom and first floors, and are no taller than that. The roofs are platforms covered either with gold or leather or even gold, but usually leather. Each family is composed of its head, his two wives, the children he has with them until the age of five, and his slaves.

There are two public houses, or rather two vast colleges, where all the children of the city are raised, boys in one, girls in the other. Here the heads of families are obliged to bring them on the first day of their sixth year; and they charge the Republic with the precious care of their education, saying in the presence of the Magistrate of the city: "Here is a citizen whom I give to the State, for him (or her) to be taught in a manner useful for it."

The Magistrate oversees these two houses, which is considered one of the most important duties of his office; as persuaded as they are that the good education of these small citizens will decide the happiness of the Republic. Widowers and widows, who have renounced further marriage are, by the choice of the Magistrate, the tutors, either of the boys or the girls. This is how they are fed and instructed. Let's discuss the boys first.

Great attention is given to their age. The younger ones usually sleep eight hours, and the rest, older than ten years, never sleep more than six. Immediately upon rising, they are made to wash in warm or cold baths, according to the season. You'd never believe how much this custom exempts them from a thousand minor illnesses, to which the children of our countries are subject: for, aside from their leaving in these baths all the filth that accumulates day and night on the skin, it seems that the medicinal herbs they add to the waters of these baths helps give all the parts of their body the sort of vigor that readies them for all sorts of labor. Then they put on their clothes, which consist in a kind of cotton shirt with trousers, and they change these every day; a cloak which hangs off them to about a foot above the ground; a cap of wool lined with a cloth of dyed cotton; and when they go out they wear a kind of light jacket. The custom that amounts to imprisoning them in the bodies of whales is unknown to them; Nature is allowed to go her way, she who never ruins her own workmanship, for among them there are no hunchbacks, or lame, or crooked legs, or stumpy feet. However, they also never wrap them in swaddling clothes, as mothers and nannies do in our countries.

Once they are dressed, they begin their exercises, the first of which is reading and writing, followed by a light meal consisting of a bit of bread and a few refreshing fruits, with which they take a glass of beer which is necessarily different according to their age. This breakfast is followed by a rougher sort of exercise: the young are made to take rather long walks in the countryside, where, on the pretext of entertainment, they tear up all the weeds scattered among the new wheat shoots. The older ones do various exercises, some riding horses, others wrestling, still others learning to skilfully fire arrows: exercises through which they pass successively. They are also sometimes led into the woods: there, some of them hunt, and others help the citizens to gather wood. When they notice the sun approaching their meridian, they return home, where a frugal dinner awaits them. They are served, first a kind of soup or rather a bouillon, made from the juice of many sorts of meats cooked together with rice: this dish is served every day. After this bouillon is distributed by measure according to age, they are served a plate of roast or fish. Before eating this, or after the meal, they drink a large glass of the same beer as in the morning; which is their dinner. After which they are given the space of a good hour for their recreation, which is passed singing or playing instruments which are quite similar to ours. But they don't know these lascivious and enchanting airs that are so much to the taste of our young folk. Their music is in no way effeminate, and their songs are only kinds of odes that contain either an elegant summary of the history of their country, or due praise to virtue, or recitals of the wonders of Nature. Here are a few I've learned, although they're in verse in the Ajaoian language, I will be content to give them in prose.

AN ODE ON THE FOUNDATION OF THE REPUBLIC OF AJAO.

More than forty thousand moons ago, our fathers, our wise fathers, tired of living among peoples whose barbaric ways were so odious, and whose views were superstition itself, sacrificing to statues of gold and silver which they called the masters of their fate; our fathers, our wise fathers, departed these Nations, and Nature bore them upon her waters, with the aid of her winds, to the land of Ajao. O happy colony! Happy fathers of a blessed people! We owe you all our tranquility! We owe you all the sweetness of our life! We owe you all the purity of our ways! Children, let us imitate such fathers: Children, let us sing their praises: to imitate them is to praise them. Children, let's imitate them: may their race last as long as Nature, forever!

AN ODE ON VIRTUE.

How happy are those who do what is right! A tranquil heart is their reward. They enjoy, as long as they see the sun, the sweetness of peace. The homeland loves them as her dearest children; they are her glory. How glorious to be loved by such a mother! Let us win her love, O children of Ajao. Virtue is what she loves! Let justice, let modesty, let temperance, let wisdom shine in all our deeds: for the homeland loves these virtues. Children of Ajao, let us be virtuous, our days will be happier for it!

ODE ON THE MARVELS OF NATURE.

Thy laws are amazing, O nursemaid of humans and of all beings! From thy generous hands come all our blessings. O Nature, Nature, our loving mother! Who can sing worthily of the greatness of thy works? Let us be worthy of the blessings of such a mother, who gives us our being, and who looks after us as long as we can be capable of enjoying these blessings and contemplating these marvels, this alternation of the seasons, these beings which give us heat, and give life to this whole uninterrupted production of beings made by one another. The greenery of the fields cheers our eyes, the tincture of the heavens attracts our glance, the singing of the birds delights our ears; all in Nature, and Nature herself, always like herself, shows us her eternity. Let us give her all our admiration.

This is what most of the Ajaoian songs are like; they know nothing of songs that are bacchic, amorous and dubious, which have always been and which remain popular in our Europe, where they serve to corrupt both sexes, from their earliest youth. From this we can judge that the rest of their diversions, that is, their recreations, are moderate and upright.

After this good and necessary amusement, those who are old enough to learn some trade will go to work with teachers in the city; and these are usually their fathers, whose profession they customarily embrace. Those who remain are kept busy reading and writing during this time, and all of them go to the refectory at sunset. There they make a light dinner, which consists of cooked vegetables (for they never eat raw ones) and fruits. This meal is followed by further recreation, after which they go to bed.

The girls are raised in the same way as to nutrition, but their exercises are sex-appropriate; and without mentioning needlework, which they all learn, great care is taken to teach them, when they are 15 to 16 years old, to become mothers of households, that is, to lead their homes with the tasks which the Ajaoians give to their women. But, above all, they are taught to have a true bond with the man who will choose them for his wife, and to study all that might contribute to make his life sweet and pleasant, and to compensate for the troubles occasioned by life's necessities. I forgot to mention that, although all the Ajaoians are highly literate, great care is taken not to teach them to write: since this seemed very odd to me, I couldn't help asking the reason for this, and all I've been able to learn is that people should give their time only to what is useful and necessary, and that writing is completely useless for women, who have no involvement with the government or the justice system. I confess that I didn't find this custom entirely mistaken; and that, if it had been received from all time, in our own country, we might have even greater respect for the opposite sex, which wouldn't have felt the itch to set itself up as Authors, which would have hidden many flaws from us. We will now leave these seminaries of citizens, to speak of the citizens themselves.

CHAPTER V: ON THE DIFFERENT MAGISTRATES OF THE AJAOIANS.

As mentioned above, each house holds twenty families. The heads of each family, which are called "Minches", choose two of themselves, who, by this choice, acquire the name of "Minchist" and carry out inspections of the whole house. Each of these Minchists or superior heads, keeps this job for two years, and one of them is changed every year, or rather, as these peoples reckon time, every fourteen moons. The forty Minchists of twenty neighboring houses gather as soon as they have been chosen, and select two of themselves, which are called "Minchiskoa", and who have duties of inspection over these forty Minchists. Therefore, since each quarter of the city of Ajao contains 800 houses, each quarter contains 80 Minchiskoa or directors of twenty houses. The Minchiskoa gather in the common house of their quarter and elect, with a plurality of votes, two elder Minchiskoa, who by this election become "Minchiskoa-Adoë", who form the city council, which selects four of the wisest and most prudent of those who have been Minchiskoa-Adoë during the previous years, to send them to the assembly of the States; and they are twenty-four Deputies of the States which form the Supreme Magistracy, before which I've appeared and which I mentioned in my first chapter.

These Minchiskoa-Adoë, Deputies to the Supreme Council, assume the title of "Adoë-Resi". They keep this office for six years: but only two of them are changed out every three years, so that the two who remain in charge can instruct the new Deputies on the state of affairs.

Minch is a lifelong calling, but when someone has passed through one of these other offices, they are rarely elected a second time; for, they do what they can to elevate each citizen in turn to these honors, so that everyone is made worthy of being called to them: a custom which produces so much emulation with all the citizens that all of them keep their conduct above reproach, to avoid the shame of seeing younger men than themselves elected in their own quarter.

CHAPTER VI: THE POLICIES OF THE AJAOIANS.

Thine and *mine* are ignored in the Island of Ajao: however, everything there is not absolutely in common. Nobody owns lands privately. This belongs to the State, which oversees its cultivation and the distribution of its fruits to each family. Here is how they provide for this cultivation. As soon as a boy has entered into his twentieth year, he is obliged to marry on pain of infamy, and being forced into a marriage by the Magistrate, and he can't wait until he is twenty-two. Even though this law is as ancient as the State itself, there is no example of its ever being broken; and a boy is careful, when he reaches his twentieth year, to select his two wives; he usually marries both of them on the same day.

The young newlyweds don't stay in the city: they immediately take their wives to the country, to the village where the Minchiskoa-Adoë, in whose presence they are married, assigns their residence; in which matter the Minchiskoa-Adoë take into account the size of the lands that depend on the villages of their districts, and the number of plowmen who are in each village: for precise registers are kept of all these things. The newlyweds populate the villages of the district of their city, of which they are all considered citizens; and they govern themselves in these villages nearly the same as in the city: for they have Minchists which they themselves elect, and who elect the Minchiskoa, who answer to the

Minchiskoa-Adoë of the city, to whom they give a precise report, every nine moons, of all that has gone one in their village.

These newlyweds populate the countryside and are responsible for agriculture. As soon as a Minch of the city reaches 75 years of age, he departs to spend the rest of his days in the country, where each village has a quarter called "the quarter of the elderly", where they are well looked after. Then the Minchiskoa-Adoë call, to replace these elders and those who die, the oldest Minchs in the country who are under sixty, since these are still young enough to work: the Ajaoians having no respect in their elections either for status or favor, because virtue alone gives them a right to the highest posts, of which they all make themselves capable.

There are public granaries and storehouses in each city and in each village, and from these they bring fruits and grains to the city, as the Minchiskoa-Adoë judge necessary. It's the same with all other provisions. There are public fishers, hunters, butchers, bakers. All of these provisions are carried to the city, always in equal quantities, into the markets, where there people are set in place by the Minchiskoa-Adoë to distribute them to each quarter. The Minchiskoa have them distributed to each house, and the Minchists to each family. This occurs every four days; it all happens in less than two hours in an orderly fashion.

It's the same with the clothes. The Minchiskoa-Adoë oversee the production of certain quantities of materials each year, and for the distribution to happen in about the same way as the foodstuffs, that is, that, when someone needs a robe, a cloak, or a pair of trousers (for this is all they wear), he goes to request it from the Minchists, who give it to him straight away.

The other needful things, of less importance, such as furniture, cooking utensils, shoes, caps, can all be purchased through barter. This custom makes everyone apply themselves to their profession, so they won't lack for anything. The same policy is observed in the country. Aside from the fact that many people simply enjoy looking out for one another's needs, as would be expected with a population who are all brethren, recognizing a common mother to whom they owe their existence; so that, if those of a single house who are of different professions see that anyone lacks for anything, they step in to offer it to him personally, indeed reserving the right to ask him for something else when needed. It will even frequently happen that, when an individual has need of something which is available from someone else, who had no need of anything he might give in exchange, he won't fail to obtain it. In short, they take genuine pleasure in mutual obligation, and this spirit is predominant among all the inhabitants of the Island. This shouldn't surprise us, they're used to it, this is how they're raised.

I've said elsewhere that the mines were public. There is no Ajaoian who doesn't make at least one pilgrimage to admire the environs of these miracles of Nature, and to take away as much as he feels he needs. The inhabitants of the district of Kaluki work mostly in the preparation of metals; for they have very few arable lands; and they trade them with travelers for other things that they bring from other districts; without realizing that every seven moons they will send a certain quantity thereof to the storehouses of the five other cities.

CHAPTER VII: ON THE FUNCTIONS OF THE MINCHISTS, THE MINCHISKOA, THE MINCHISKOA-ADOË, THE ADOE-REZI.

These four sorts of Magistrates, each of which is subordinate to the other, are charged with all the weight of the Government, of the Police, of the Justice system, of the upkeep of the population.

The Minchiskoa-Adoë have the most difficult duty, for they are like fathers of a vast district, the families of which they must feed and govern. They keep precise registers of births and deaths in all their dependency; for there is an infinity of things which, among them, are dependent on age. They have another register of the sizes of the lands of their district and of each village, of how they should be planted and their proportional interrelations; another register of those who are in each profession, since the number of those who should embrace it is related to the advantage each profession brings to the State.

I will say in passing that the trades that are most in vogue among the Ajaoians are those of plowmen (which everyone does), weavers, bakers, fishers, butchers, metalworkers, boiler-workers (who make all the vessels from gold or silver), carpenters, masons, cobblers, brewers, armorers, and woodcutters. They have neither doctors, nor surgeons, nor cooks, nor pastry chefs, nor tailors (each woman makes all the clothes for her family), nor lawyers, nor sergeants, nor notaries. Some of these professions are entirely unknown to them, and they consider the rest as useless or detrimental to society. Indeed, what could be more useless, not to say harmful, than medicine? Is there any doctor, capable as you like, who could boast of prolonging the life of a man by a single minute? Their art is rather an honest charlatanism than a certain science, and it's well known that they can rightly be called the privileged and exempted murderers of justice. Cooks and pastry chefs should not be tolerated in any State where the health of the subjects is of any concern, which they are so good at ruining with the delicacy of their seasonings. As for men of the robe, they are clearly useless for the Ajaoians, who live as brothers to each other, and who have nothing of their own. But even if this weren't so, these sorts of people have so little conscience and such greed that they are the plague of society, and the fatal torch that continually sparks the fire of discord. But enough with my thoughts, let's get back to the subject.

The Minchiskoa-Adoë are careful to ensure that nobody is idle, and that agriculture is carefully attended to, and that the youth are raised properly. These are their three great tasks. They send orders to the Minchiskoa of the villages, to send the necessary provisions to the city, and to send the excess from one village to another which lacks something. And if by some accident some city and its district are missing something necessary, they send word to the Minchiskoa-Adoë of the five other cities, which work together to provide from the superfluous quantity they have. Yet, as these Minchiskoa-Adoë keep, as it were, the Assizes, that is, they receive complaints and remonstrances of each individual, who might appear without fear, and speak as freely as a Polish man in the Diets, or an Englishman in Parliament; and immediately the Minchiskoa-Adoë, taking the matter into consideration, remedy matters according to the demands of prudence: by this means, peace and tranquility are maintained in the State; and the people can only blame their own nonchalance and timidity if they lack anything or if things are out of order.

On another day they go to visit the "Miakarezi", or the public houses, which includes those of the young people, the hospitals, the houses of the slaves, and the public warehouses, to see if everything is in order there, and if the inspectors of these places are performing their duties; and when they find them lacking, they take all their duties from them, which is a true burden, and they become notorious by this deposition, because they have failed in the service they owe to the Republic. Thus, since honor and self-interest are the motives of all their actions, we shouldn't be astonished if they're rarely found in the wrong, and if these two motives do for them what the fear of a terrifying God does for us.

Each Minchist surveys all that happens in the house of which he's the Minchist, and then does all he can to ensure that everything is peaceful there. If any disorder comes about, the Minchists do their best to remedy it, invoking their authority, which is always very moderate, before things get out of hand. But when they foresee no success, they give a report to the Minchiskoa, who accompany the Mlnchists to visit the individuals concerned, who committed the crime or disorder, examine their reasons, and condemn to irons those who deserve it, or even to slavery, according to the grievousness of the crime: sometimes even, although this is quite rare, they condemn to a corporal punishment that could be called bastonnade; but they never condemn to death, since, they say, it is against nature and reason to take from a creature something you can't give it; and that, by taking the life of a criminal known for this crime, this would be the greatest service you could give him, by taking away his infamy and remorse, these normal effects of crime. This is also the reason why their law ordains that, if any citizen in the Republic is so denatured and wicked as to make an attempt on the life or the honor of one of his fellow-citizens, he will be condemned to become the slave of he who would have been dishonored, or of the parents of he whose life he would have taken, and he won't be allowed to have children, for fear that he might beget monsters like himself; and to make him known to all men, the name of his crime is written on his forehead, with the indelible juice of certain plants. But, no such monster has been seen to date in the whole Island of Ajao. Living like brothers, they never have quarrels, and they don't even have a word for vengeance. Other crimes that might be more common there, such as laziness, disobedience to the orders of one's superiors, negligence of one's domestic duties, are punished by the Minchiskoa, as I've said: but the worst punishment that follows the one inflicted by the Minchiskoa, is that the condemned party thereby becomes incapable of performing any public function; and the names of all the condemned remain exposed in the public square on a kind of column for 700 moons, where the name, family, and quarter of the condemned is put on display. But, it must be confessed that these condemnations are quite rare, and that during the five years I've lived in Ajao, I've seen only four names of the condemned on the criminal column; so observant the Ajaoians truly are of their law.

The role of the Adoë-Rezi is the most thorny and difficult of all. Sixteen Minchiskoa-Adoë are charged with the government of a city and its district; but the twenty-four Adoë-Rezi are charged with that of the six cities and their districts; while the Supreme Council oversees affairs of war and peace, of money, roadways, public buildings, and the compensation that is sometimes necessary between districts, in case of unequal harvests. This Supreme Magistrate is also the trustee of the laws he must see observed in the whole Republic. Finally, all the unusual occurrences, such as our shipwreck, are brought before this Supreme Council, which resides at Ajao and decides all matters on the spot, with a plurality of votes.

The Adoë-Rezi, or the Councilor-Deputies, assemble every day, from sunrise to midday, in the palace I've just given a slight idea of. This is a large edifice, where each Adoë-Rezi has his apartment in which he resides with his family, which he brings to stay in Ajao during the six years he resides there.

These twenty-four Adoë-Rezi form four Councils: 1. that of the law, which delivers justice; 2. that of lands, which oversees the revenue of each year, of the ameliorations and changes in cultivation; 3. that of buildings, which sees to the maintenance of the public buildings of all cities, and of the roadways, ports, and coasts of the whole Island; 4. that of the finances, of war, and of peace.

There is a great hall in the palace, alongside which there are four chambers, where these four Councils hold their assemblies; and when any unusual business requires a compromise, the four Committees present themselves at the hall of the Supreme Council, where these 24 Deputies are seated in a circle on a kind of mat, the same as are found in all the houses of Ajao, and which is made of a kind of rush that is very supple and of various colors.

In the middle of the circle, which has no President, are four large books, which I mentioned in the first chapter, in which each Adoë-Rezi has a right to record the resolutions taken in the full assembly; for they have neither secretary nor clerk, liable as these are to modify a decree to the advantage of the highest bidder. These books never leave the hall of the Council, where each Adoë-Rezi can consult them during the sitting. Aside from these registers, each Council has its own where it inscribes all its resolutions. This, then, is the orderliness with which the whole Republic is governed in the most tranquil manner on earth.

CHAPTER VIII. ON WAR, ON THE TREASURY, THE SLAVES, AND THE POLITICS OF THE AJAOIANS.

I will say nothing about the three committees of the law, lands, and buildings: everyone will easily conceive which things pertain to each of these. I will only touch on the fourth, which is that of war, of peace and of finances; because, having shown on one hand that the Ajaoians are, as it were, separate from the rest of mankind, given the location of their Island, and on the other that they have no money, it comes naturally to mind that this fourth council would be quite useless; but this would be a mistake, as will be seen: for all that I will say in this chapter, relates to this Council.

The most common opinion among the Ajaoians about their origin, is that they came from China or Tartary, and that their ancestors only abandoned their homeland to go live in some unpopulated land, to escape a tyrannical government and superstition, and to form, in this new homeland, the sort of government they wanted, and a Religion free of prejudice and superstition.

This opinion is based on some old Odes, similar to the first one I shared in Chap. IV, and some others in a language nearly unknown to the Ajaoians, and which is very similar to that of the inhabitants of Piantsoy and Subatzey, which are two provinces of greater Tartary, towards the sea of the Kaïmakites.

From this it can be concluded that the first Ajaoians were a colony of people quite similar to those who are now called *esprits forts*, that is, people with no other prejudice than that of submitting in all their conduct to the dictates of sound reason, enlightened by constant attentiveness to the duties which Nature impressed on us as necessary, in giving us our being.

Having departed from whatever country it was, which they concealed from their descendants, maybe for good reasons, they landed on the Island they called Ajao, the previous name of which is unknown to us. This Island was populated in part by a rather indolent people, whom the Ajaoians pursued as far as the mountains of Kalusti; they forced them all to submit without terms, men, women and children.

They enslaved all of them, and, having passed them in review, they found that they were too numerous to have anything to fear from them; thus they killed all those who were over 50. They saved 1000 grown men, about that many boys from the earliest age, all the women still young enough for childbearing, and the young girls: and soon after, when the whole Island was surveyed, and a division into six parts was made, which remains to this day, they divided these slaves among the inhabitants of the six cities.

Since these newcomers didn't have enough women with them to populate the Island quickly, they married many of their captives above the age of 24, and placed many young girls in the educational houses of the citizens, to efface any knowledge of their slavery; and the citizens later married them.

As for the other slaves, a chain is placed on their neck and leg. There is a law by which it was ordained that they would belong to nobody in particular, but only to the State; that each male slave could have only one wife; that no slave would marry before the age of thirty-two, and any who had a child before this time would be condemned to death along with their child (but this law was mitigated and the death penalty was changed to perpetual imprisonment); that no slave, man or woman, would in the future marry with citizens; that of the male children born to slave women in the course of 14 moons or a year, only the number of males would be allowed to live who were double the number of males who died the previous year, and that the superfluous ones would be smothered at birth; but that all the girls would be allowed to live.

That this latter article of the law was contrary to Nature, is something I recognize; and I don't doubt that, by driving these former inhabitants out of their country, by reducing them to slavery, and wielding this inhumane law against their children, the ancient Ajaoians themselves must have condemned what politics forced them to do. But it was inadvisable to allow too much power to a population they didn't want to destroy, and at the same time prevent it from growing large enough to avenge itself one day, through its descendants, for the offense received by their ancestors. They could only do this by means of this law, which, as inhumane as it seems, is as gentle as could be done in such a circumstance.

Each quarter of the city contains an Ergastule, where the slaves of the quarter, men and women, are shut in at night an hour after sundown. These Ergastules are very spacious and contain many small rooms, with four beds each, and where these slaves are rather at their ease. Their clothes are made like those of their masters, but the color is different; and the slaves of each quarter wear different colors. It is forbidden for the slaves of one quarter to mingle with those of another quarter, and any citizen who sees this happening has a right to give them a whipping on the spot. They no longer wear the chain on their necks, it's now attached, for greater comfort, below the left knee and above the right elbow, going behind the waist.

Finally, there are buildings in the countryside where they raise their children, just as those of the citizens are raised in the city: the one for boys is in one village, and the one for girls is in another; and, as soon as they are old enough to provide some service, they are placed with the citizens of the countryside who need them, from whom they are taken and moved to the city as needed. Finally, the law of suffocation was abolished; and, in what follows, I will say what is done with the boy slaves when too many are seen in the Island. All these things are the business of the Committee of War.

All these details of the invasion of the Island and the misfortune of its inhabitants are handed down from father to son in a kind of little poem, which these slaves carefully teach their children in their original language, despite the express prohibitions of the Ajaoians, who do all they can to suppress in the memory of these unfortunates what happened to their fathers.

Although the Ajaoians are separated from all other men, as it were, by the position of their Island, they would seem to have no reason to fear that anyone will come to disturb their peace, and yet they keep on foot a militia without parallel in our Europe. Since, on one hand, they are not unaware of the eagerness of the Europeans to seize the wealth of others, and that on the other, experience convinces them that others might find the way to their Island just as they themselves once found it, that is, by chance, which happened to me too along with a few others; they have thought it to the prudence and welfare of the State to always be ready to repel force with force: which they can do all the easier as only two beaches to the west, that of Jaroi and Ajao, are accessible. But, even without these reasons, it would be prudent for them to always be on guard, even against the original inhabitants, their slaves.

This militia is composed only of married men, from the age of 22 to 50, and it includes all the citizens, who are divided by companies, in each village and in each quarter of the city, and by brigades of each district. The companies assemble once each moon, and the Minchiskoa, who are their captains, review and drill them: and every year, that is, at the end of the fourteenth moon, all the companies assemble in a kind of Champ de Mars close to each city, where they camp for two days; and, on the third day the Minchiskoa-Adoë lead them near lake Fu in the province of Lamo, where the Adoë-Rezi are present to pass in review all the citizens of the Island, who then celebrate certain military games, in which prizes of honor are awarded. These feasts last seven days, after which each new Magistrate enters the office to which he has been named before departing the city or village; and before this army separates, the public is given a sight of those who have been condemned to infamy.

During this voyage all the men slaves follow the camp with the food and tents, which are of a reddish color and of a kind of waxed cotton; and the women stay at home, cleaning it during their husband's absence.

Although, in the description of Ajao, I said that this Island seemed remote from all the coasts of either continent, the inhabitants seem to fear the arms of a Nation to their east, and with which there is some appearance that they have already had some war, from what I've been able to learn. I haven't been able to discover what Nation this is, unless it's the Northern Californians, or the Americans who live above Mexico and who haven't yet been contacted. However this may be, the Ajaoians are strongly on guard against this Nation: they don't seek it out, but if it should attack them, they are always prepared for it, and to keep it from their shores, along with all other enemies.

This is the place to explain in passing, by what adventure we found ourselves in the Island of men who spoke Dutch. Since the Ajaoians are a colony that came from our continent, we shouldn't ask whether they are aware that they aren't the only inhabitants of the universe, as the inhabitants of a certain pacific island, discovered in our times, thought; aside from this, prior to our arrival they had already seen many ships wrecked on the reefs surrounding their Island. The ancient Ajaoians knew how cautious one must be against the human mob, and that they might see themselves some day exposed to the same treatment as they had inflicted on the aborigines of their Island. To prevent any surprise, they are careful to occasionally send some of the most prudent of their citizens to neighboring States, especially to Tartary, China and Japan. These envoys, or rather spies, are very careful to examine, above all, whether there is any talk of their Island and what might be said of it; and they have direct orders to apply themselves diligently to discover the practices of those they suspect might have designs on their country.

Since these spies have learned, on their various travels, of the greed of the French, the Portuguese, the Spanish and the Dutch to discover new lands, to seize them without any right, the war committee, etc. has sent some with orders to go as far as Goa, Madagascar, Batavia, to watch out for the interests of their homeland. It's in these principal cities of eastern Asia where they learn all the languages of our Europe and of Asia.

There are always 12 ships in the ports of Ajao and Jaroi, which are carefully maintained, both for a perpetual state of preparation for the defense of the island from without, and to transport these envoys at need, to the shores of China, from where they go into other countries wearing Chinese clothes and speaking their language, which is the first one they learn after departing their country. From these envoys the Ajaoians have gained a perfect knowledge of what goes on in Europe and Asia, the wars that transpire there, the revolutions that happen, and the ways of nearly all Nations; of these they keep precise records, which they have the young people to read in the educational houses. But, whatever esteem is had for these envoys, when they return to their country they aren't given any public duties, since it's rightly feared that, having seen so many bad examples in their travels, they might put them into practice to the detriment of the liberties of their fellow-citizens.

The ships that lead these spies to the shores of Asia, also carry all the young slave boys judged superfluous by the committee of war. They are put ashore on the first coast where they think they can do so without being seen, and they are abandoned to their fate, for better or worse. This treatment seemed softer than suffocation at birth. Those who are destined for this fate are raised in such a way that they are unaware if there are any other men on earth than them; and they are no older than twelve when they are taken away, so that they can't inform the people they meet, either of their country or its government.

The war committee sees that the Minchiskoa-Adoë of each village are maintaining a certain number of coast guard, who watch day and night from the height of the large towers built on the seaside, to see if any ship is coming to disturb the tranquility of this happy State. These are the sentinels who found us; and soon after, the whole brigade of the district of Ajao had taken up arms, a part of which appeared at the coast. The alarm had even spread across the whole Island, which didn't keep anyone from receiving us with great humanity, because they saw that we hadn't come to do any harm. But, in all truth, we were lucky to have been separated from our ships of war, for if they had been any closer, we wouldn't have been forgiven, and we would have fallen into a miserable enslavement: which was the fate of a hundred Japanese explorers; since they hadn't been able to manage as well as us, they paid with their liberty for the greed of discovery.

It might rightly be asked what the Ajaoians do with this treasure, which I mentioned while describing the fortress and lake of Fu. This proper curiosity must be satisfied. Firstly, this treasury contains immense sums of gold and silver, minted with the stamp and arms of China and Japan; and there is no year when they don't beat ten million pounds of gold, taken for the public from the mine of Kei. This gold is given to those who are sent to spy among their neighbors. But, the main use of these treasures is to buy the support of the Chinese or Japanese, in case either of these two nations, or some other one, has designs on the Island of Ajao; these peoples, not ignorant of the jealousy that reigns among nearby peoples, and what manner of machinery gold is capable of setting in motion, they put these two means to use for the preservation of their liberty.

This treasure is in a fortress built by Nature on the summit of a mountain, in the middle of the vast lake formed by the confluence of three rivers. If it is kept in this spot, it's not because of any fear that individuals might steal it; even if heaped in the public square it would be safe, since they could go and take as much from the mines if they wanted it. This is so that the enemies, if any should appear, won't be able to seize it, and to keep the slaves from seizing it, to use against the State that which is meant for the welfare thereof.

CHAPTER IX: ON MARRIAGE AND CHILDBEARING.

I've already said that it is ordained, on pain of infamy, for every young man who reaches the age of twenty, to get married. This law has never been broken. Because all the impediments that might arise among us are unknown to the Ajaoians; among them none are languid, or mutilated, or *refrigidis* and *maleficiatis*.

The education, the choice of foods given to the young, obviate these obstacles. Rarely will you find any girls who aren't nubile before the age of 16; but they can't get married before they turn 18. Thus, when a young man reaches his 20th year, he sets his glance on those with whom he wants to spend the rest of his days. This choice is usually made in the days of amusement, at the renewal of all moons; then, all the young boys and girls go walking at the same spot, with their chaperones. There, these novices of love give their first sighs; and when an admirer declares himself to a pretty girl, he has the right, if his declaration is accepted, to go during his free time to pay his respects to his mistress, in the girls' Minkarezi, where there are visiting chambers quite similar to the parloirs of the Nuns in Flanders, except for the grilles. There, a prudish *Cupid* takes pleasure in firing all his quiver at these young and tender hearts. Quite often, the boy sees his two mistresses in these chambers at the same time; to habituate them early on to living and getting along with him. For, as I've said, each

Ajaoian must have two wives; a law which was wisely established to make home life less disagreeable for the citizens, in that these two wives, disputing in a kind fashion, to keep the husband's love, they avoid causing him the sort of sorrow which are so common in countries where a single wife is often more the mistress of the house than the poor husband, whose life is a tissue of sorrows, or rather, a true hell.

Eight days before a young man wants to marry, he declares his wishes to the superiors of the educational house, who lead him before the MInchiskoa, who bring the father and mother of the girl, if they are alive, or one of the two or, in their absence, the Minchist of their house; and the young man tells them in the presence of the Minchiskoa: "Nature, having preserved me to an age where I could give citizens to the State, I have chosen your daughter, ... to be one of my companions, for your good pleasure, if she is without physical defects which might lead to the State having malformed citizens."

The father, if he consents, takes his daughter's right hand in his left, and with his right on top of the young man's right, replies: "Since your hearts are in agreement, we unite you: may Nature make you the father of a large family." Then, the mother leads her daughter, who, from this moment, leaves the educational house forever. She places under her outer robe a kind of shirt of a fabric clearer than gauze. When she is in the presence of her lover, the Minchiskoa withdraw for a moment along with the father, and the mother, removing the girl's outer robe, gives her future son in law a glance, through the gauze, of all the charms that Nature placed on the body of her daughter. The ceremony for the other one is usually performed on the same day, to prevent any arguments about priority.

Eight days after the young man leaves the educational house, after receiving a ticket from the Minchiskoa-Adoë, assigning his residence in the country, he comes to the house where he was born where he is given a room: the fathers of his mistresses lead him, accompanied by the Minchists of their house. This ceremony is performed after sundown; and the young man lies between the two women in the presence of those who brought them, who close the door of the chamber, and depart to register this marriage. The next day the newly married man departs for the countryside where he will form his new home.

When a woman senses the moment she will give birth, she sends for two women from the Mins where she resides, to help her and serve as witnesses. As soon as she is delivered, the two attendants bring her husband into the room, and if it's a boy his wife has delivered, they present him to him, after he has been washed in warm water, with the words: "Behold a citizen with whom Nature has favored your wife; rejoice in him and raise him for the Republic." If it's a girl, they only point to her, saying: "Behold she whose father you are."

Mothers are always the wetnurses of their own children, unless there is some impediment, in which case the wives of the Mins who can serve as wetnurses will volunteer for the job. Boys are only nursed for eight months, and girls ten; because the former are encouraged to form, from their tenderest youth, a nature that is robust and suited to physical labor; whereas the girls, being destined only for domestic work, can be raised somewhat more delicately. I pass on to the subject which puts an end to everything.

CHAPTER X: ON DEATH AND FUNERALS.

Since the Island of Ajao is also part of the same planet, it should cause no shock that the disorder of the elements cause the same evils there as in other countries. However, during my five years residing here, I've noted that they suffer from no diseases other than fever, which they might get rid of with a few bleedings, if this custom were established. But when they fall ill, they only revise their diet and leave the rest to Nature, who doesn't fail to preserve her workmanship; so that these happy mortals observe from childhood a great dietary regime of life, and indulge in none of our delicacies of taste, they never die before the age of 80 or 90.

When an old man of this age falls ill, nobody expects he will heal; instead, his relatives who are close to hand come to his bedside to hear his last words. They ask him about the most remarkable things he saw in his life; and they ask his advice on the defects he might have found in society. Usually each elderly person prepares a short speech for this last moment, where he briefly recapitulates his whole life, and exhorts his loved ones to uphold the liberty he enjoyed, and to transmit the same to posterity, just as he passed it to them. When he senses the approach of his final hour, a Minchiskoa is notified, to whom he says the following: "I was born on such and such a day, in such and such place. I return to the bosom of Nature, from which I came. I give thanks to the homeland for the blessings it has lavished on me, and the tranquility in which I passed my days under its protection. I leave it citizens of my own blood, who will only render themselves worthy of its parentage by doing what I have done for it: if they do so, I commend them to it with all my heart."

After this grateful farewell, they wait for death peacefully; anticipating their coming annihilation with a more serene gaze than a superstitious and fanatical person who pants for the frivolous delights of their supposed paradise.

As soon as they expire, the Magistrate is notified, who sets up a pyre outside the town or village, in the spot set apart for funerals: the cadaver is carried there after sundown, dressed in its normal clothing. All the Minchs of the house are the officiants. The Minchist sets fire to the pyre[28]; and once the whole is reduced to ashes, they are cast along with those of the pyre into a pit, which is made in the same place.

At this final moment and in these final duties, neither sobs nor moans, nor the crying of the parents upset at their loss, are heard. Submissive to Nature, they respect her laws and accept her orders passively. Indeed, with us these cries, these sobs are us less an effect of Nature suffering this separation (as they say), than self-interest

---

[28] On which the cadaver is within a circle of iron, the bottom of which is a sort of wire mesh.

bemoaning its loss. And as proof of this, that this Nature is rarely seen to suffer at the death of some relatives whose loss is no loss to us, or from whom we expect a large inheritance. The Ajaoian has no other relatives than the homeland: because he received all he has from it. He considers all men as beings united by Nature for a time; when she finds it suitable to withdraw them, why censure, with bitter complaints, the ways of this good mother?

The final honors paid to women and the young are precisely the same as are paid to men, but they don't include the speeches and the farewells.

CHAPTER XI: THE REST OF THE HISTORY OF THE AUTHOR'S STAY AND THAT OF HIS COMPANIONS ON THE ISLE OF AJAO.

It remains for me to inform the reader of what happened to me and my companions in this happy Republic, and how I came to leave this Island. My companions hadn't been on the Island two months before they were already saying that they were very happy with the Ajaoian morals and way of life. Some of them had some religious scruples, but they eventually followed the majority; and we asked the Supreme Magistrate what would be done with us, adding that we were ashamed to eat any more bread that we weren't earning, and for which purpose we begged him to put us to use. A council was held on this matter. I was introduced into it, and I was asked whether we agreed to renounce our own country forever, and whether we wished to be accepted as citizens of Ajao. Everyone consented cheerfully. Thus, we were naturalized on the spot; and, since none among us wasn't over the age of twenty, it was proposed that we take wives from the locals. Nobody refused this proposition. We were divided into 4 bands: one was sent to Lamo, another to Peridi, the third to Dorao, and the fourth to Jaroi. There, the Minchiskoa-Adoë led us, on the orders of the Adoë-Rezi, to the educational house of the young slaves of each city, where everyone chose two women, who were thereby given their freedom.

When the nuptials completed, each band was dispersed into the villages of the district of the city to which it had been sent; and our Europeans are so used to the customs of the country that it was very hard to distinguish them from the natives when I departed. Many had children, and they lived very well with their wives and with the other Minchs of the houses where they were residing. But there was some semblance that they would never be called to the city, even less the duties of trust.

As for me, I had contracted a close connection with Pu-ki, the Adoë-Rezi of the city of Ajao, and the brother of our interpreter: and since I was not minded to distinguish myself from my comrades in matters of marriage, I thought it fitting to start by choosing where I would base myself, and I told my friend that I would be quite happy to reside in Ajao itself. As prompt to help me as if we'd been friends for twenty years already, he obtained permission for this the next day from the Minchiskoa-Adoë; and as he said so, he smiled and told me the following: "This order of the Magistrate naturalizes you; all you now lack is two Ajaoian ladies, and then we will be sure to keep you forever. I have two daughters in the educational house, if you find them worthy of your choice, nothing will please me more than to contribute in some way to bonding you to our country: the first is called Perciki and the other Fareki, and they are both of marriageable age; you can see them on the first Jai[29]."

How could I refuse such an agreeable order? I saw the lovely daughters of Pu-ki, and eight days later they were my wives.

I soon found myself a citizen of the capital, without losing hope about playing a role in the government. Indeed, having become the father of two boys, who were born at about the same time as each other before the end of the year of marriage, I was elected one of the Minchists of my house the next year. They could see how I was connected to the homeland with bonds that were so sweet and so strong that I'd never wish to break them; nor have I ever thought of such a thing, and I consider it as my only home.

Elated by my establishment and lofty position, I still didn't give in to a thousand reflections which occasionally troubled my conscience; although I was forced to acknowledge that there was perhaps no Nation under heaven whose morals were purer, whose government was more equitable, whose laws were more just and whose tranquility was more perfect. However, this forgetting of the God, the idea of whom had been given to me by my parents and my minister, from which I saw these people suffering, made me infinitely sad, and I would have liked to become the apostle of Ajao. I shared my thoughts on this with my father-in-law, who initially laughed at me, but I eventually won him over. The difficulty was to find a way of carrying out my project. After thinking on it, I found no better plan than to give a

---

[29] This is the first day of each quarter moon.

speech on the existence of the God of the Christians, in the presence of all the Ajaoians, when on the 14th moon[30] they would all be assembled near lake Fu. My father-in-law approved of this plan. His brother, our interpreter, who had taught me the Ajaoian language, helped me polish my speech, which I shared with my father-in-law, some two moons prior to the assembly. He encouraged me to carry out such a fine project boldly, and promised to gain the permission of the Supreme Magistracy, of which he was a member, to speak of my God to their people. He did obtain this; and this is how I preached.

---

[30] As mentioned in Chapter VIII.

CHAPTER XII: A DISCOURSE ON THE EXISTENCE OF GOD, PRONOUNCED IN 1679, TO THE GENERAL ASSEMBLY OF THE PEOPLES OF AJAO, NEAR LAKE FU.

"Ajaoians, dear Compatriots, the blessings your ever-happy State has lavished upon we mortals, whom death was about to take, if you had not so humanely supported them, are so profoundly engraved in our memory, that we could find no terms strong enough to express our gratitude to you: since it is equal to the benefit provided, it must be unlimited. We cannot show it to you more openly and more loudly than in this Assembly of all your powerful Nation, with which you have so kindly integrated us, and the happiness in which you have allowed us to participate, by accepting us as citizens of your cities. But, to go beyond words alone, we want to show by our deeds, our submission to your just laws, our diligence in agriculture, and by our attentiveness to the primary education of our children, that we are no ingrates; and that, having forgotten all the vices of our former country, we have become true Ajaoians, that is, men who submit to good sense and reason, and who love nothing more than to see virtue triumphant.

"Personally, Ajaoians, you have such consideration for the rank I held among my own people, that I made every effort to recognize the distinguished favors with which you've honored me, not only by treating me so considerately after our shipwreck, but also by accepting me as a citizen of your capital city, where I'd already been honored with a dignity which is the first step in rising to the highest offices of State. It's this same ardent desire to show you my gratitude which gives me the boldness of speaking today before an entire population, the wisest, most just, most powerful, most enlightened, most virtuous, and happiest one under heaven.

"But I won't limit my gratitude to vain words, which will be carried off by the wind blowing in this plain. I want to contribute, Ajaoians, to making you a thousand times happier than you are, by teaching you the one thing you still lack for your happiness. These words will shock you, with good reason: but lend me a favorable ear, and I don't doubt that you'll lose your astonishment, to admire how it might be that you have been ignorant for so long of the great truth that I will teach you.

"You regard, O happy people, the earth, or rather, all of Nature, as your good mother; you believe that all beings receive from this Nature life, motion, and existence. You are not the first, or the only peoples with this belief; but you are the only ones who have preserved it for so long. Reason, this absolute rule of all your actions, has dissuaded all others, and they have all recognized that there is a Being from whom Nature herself derives her existence. This Being is the God of my homeland, who is worshiped in all of Asia, in most of Africa, and in some parts of America. This is the God with whom I would today acquaint you; and for this reason I will limit myself to proving to you that Nature is not eternal, that it neither made itself nor was it made by chance; and consequently, that there is a Being brought into existence by no other, a Being who gave it to all things: this Being is what I call the only God.

"That Nature is not eternal, is something she herself proclaims her newness in a thousand visible features, because she can't hide them from us. To be convinced of this, we need only carefully consider it and learn from the most ancient peoples of antiquity about their origins.

"It's a vice common to all Nations to dispute their priority with all the rest. However, if you look at the oldest monuments of the most ancient of Nations, if you study its history, if you read its annals, you'll never go back further than five or six thousand years, at most. What is this handful of years compared with eternity?

"I have made no claim that can't be proved. The Chinese, the peoples of Asia, from whom you apparently come, claim great antiquity; and yet they allow no more than 64,834 moons (4,631 years) of existence for their Empire, from its foundation by their great Emperor Fohi. The histories of the peoples of our Europe speak of nothing nearly that ancient. It is true that the Egyptians, the most ancient people of Africa, place their origin more than 1,560,000 moons ago. This is, indeed, a very long time: but even by adding millions more too, this would do nothing against the force of my argument, since a beginning would still be recognized. This avowal is universal, and there is no Nation, as vain as it may be, which dares boast of eternity. Even yours, O happy people, doesn't find its own origin beyond 40,000 moons ago. Behold, Ajaoians, all the Nations on earth concurring to destroy the eternity of the universe, by recognizing recent origins.

"But let us seek other witnesses. If the world were eternal, the invention of what is useful and necessary for life would be equally ancient. However, we see that all the arts, all the sciences, all the things men make use of, were only invented over time, and have passed from one people to another; just as peoples have passed from one climate to another, from one corner of the planet to another.

"Just like a new people, you have only the things that were known to the first men. All new peoples have had the same fate; dedication to agriculture and a praiseworthy simplicity in all things. How many arts and sciences are you ignorant of? Music is unknown to you; Medicine is not cultivated among you; Printing, which is a fine art of quickly writing even the longest books, and an infinity of other similar arts, have never entered the minds of your inhabitants. It has been the same with all new peoples: but, little by little all the sciences, all the arts have passed from one to another; can a surer proof be found of newness? For, if the world were eternal, all these things would be as ancient as itself, or at least we should be unable to mark the date of their birth, or know anything of their inventors.

"If I pronounced this discourse before an assembly of historical savants, I would go into each science and each art; and, by considering all the Nations of Asia and Europe, it would be easy to point out the era belonging to of each of them; but this would crush you under a vain erudition: and, content as I am to have proposed you these two certain proofs of the newness of the universe, I don't doubt that, making a proper use of your reason, you will agree with me in concluding that the universe clearly had a beginning.

"If it had a beginning, then who made it? This question naturally follows the conclusion we have drawn from I proved. It has only two solutions: either the world was made by chance, or some Being made it; for, to claim that it formed itself is an absurdity undeserving of refutation.

"But, as all of Nature has preached its newness to us, even so all that is in Nature informs us that it was not made by chance: but here I need to explain what is meant by chance.

"Let's assume that you have a sack full of all kinds of seeds. You spill it in a field, and each grain of seed landed with those of its own species: all the wheat was planted together, all the rice together, all the oats together, and so on; you might say that this sowing happened by chance. This is a comparison. Let's reason, and examine whether the universe might have been made in the same way. I maintain the opposite, and I need only set before your eyes the fabrication of all creatures, to make you agree that I'm on the side of truth.

"This sun, the flame of which is always so bright, shines so temperately on us and so regularly, how could it have been placed at such a perfect distance from us that, if it were a little further its fire would be useless to us, if it were closer it would be uncomfortable and even dangerous, if only chance led to its formation and its well-regulated movement? Remember what chance is, and how the operations of this blind power, or rather this nothing, are as imaginary as itself: see that chance cannot be its cause.

"But, let us cast our eyes on something more palpable: let's examine ourselves. All these parts of our body, so well matched and placed with such grand order in the precise spot to serve the whole individual, without interfering with each other, these bones so artistically fitted together, these muscles, this flesh which covers them, these nerves which are like springs making it all move, these veins carrying life to all these parts, this skin, finally, which covers all these things, and which defend them from so many accidents which some disorder might cause: are these the operations, is that the workmanship of a blind chance which, without rule or intelligence, is supposed to have formed, compassed, and arranged all these things? Can such an absurd thought even occur to anyone's mind? What I say of the sun and of man, applies to animals, plants, metals, in a word, to all Nature's parts; to a tree, a flower, a simple plant, where all is amazing, everything proclaims the power and shows the hand of its maker.

"Let us therefore confess, Ajaoians, that this chance, as a blind being, or rather as nothing at all, cannot reasonably be credited with the formation of Nature. It remains, then, to recognize a Being, the maker of this universe. It's this same Being that I proclaim to you, it's this Being I exhort you to recognize as the author of your existence. Since it is evident from what has been said that there must be a Being who made all things, it follows that he was prior to all things, and that, having given existence to all, he received his own from nobody else: for, if he had received it from another he would have had a predecessor, which is incompatible with what we have already agreed on. Let us, therefore, conclude that this Being had no beginning, that he is eternal. His works, the whole universe, proclaim his omnipotence which is infinite, and it is by this omnipotence that he formed all things, or rather that he created them; for if he had only formed them, we would have to posit a pre-existing matter, which is absurd; but his mighty hand made matter from nothing, and with it he formed all the beings the universe is composed of.

"From the nature of these beings, we can draw conclusion about the nature of he who made them; and there is nobody who, while admiring the order and beauty of the creatures, will fail to recognize the supreme wisdom of the Creator, an attribute which is not compatible with matter. And, Ajaoians, there is nobody among you who, reflecting deeply, will not realize that neither his flesh, nor his brain, nor his blood thinks, and that there is inside us something that performs this function: this something, my wise Compatriots, is what is called spirit or mind. And the nature of this great God is that of a Spirit, an intelligent Being, which does nothing except by reason and for reason. Can you find anything so great in Nature? Who among you doesn't sense that while we are here on the plain of Fu, this something which thinks within him, goes into a thousand places in a single instant, where his body would take a long time to go: some are here in their bodies while their minds are at Jaroi, at Ajao, or elsewhere. Those among you, who have crossed the sea and visited the Nations who worship this great God, are currently traveling among these Nations, and remembering all they have seen done for the worship of this Supreme Being. Such is this great God: he is everywhere, in a moment; and since he's a far more perfect spirit than ours which is contained in the prison of our body, he is everywhere at the same time: in short, he is immense and infinite; and by this attribute he oversees the order you see predominant in the universe, and this is his venerated Providence. Could such a Being be anything other than just, clement, beneficent, to those creatures he himself has fashioned? All these glorious and great attributes must win our respect, our worship, our love. Set up altars to him, O happy people, he is the source of your blessings, from him you have this happy simplicity, this astute equity, this incomparable charity, which makes you so agreeable in his sight! Thank him for such great blessings, pay tribute to him; and be assured that, by cultivating the virtues of your Ancestors, he will lavish his blessings on you, will defend you from all your enemies, and will make you the happiest people on earth!"

I had hardly finished my speech when I noticed a great commotion among the leaders of the assembly, who immediately dispersed. Everyone withdrew to their tents, and I had the satisfaction, in the company of my father-in-law, of being complimented by many of the Minchiskoa-Adoë, on whose minds I had made a certain impression. I was even told that the Adoë-Rezi were planning an extraordinary assembly, in the afternoon, to deliberate on my speech; and that, without a doubt, they would summon me for clarifications, and ask my opinion on the way of worshiping the true God, and establishing his cult among this people.

I was impatient to receive this message, especially while they were holding council; but this was in vain. That evening, I learned from my father-in-law that, after much deliberation, they were about to take a resolution corresponding to my hopes when Puki-haï, the Adoë-Rezi of the city of Lamo, who had previously traveled in Asia, and from there to Europe, had traveled through Italy, France, Germany, and England, begged his colleagues to take things slowly, and to allow him a speech in response to mine, after which they would be better able to come to a proper resolution.

My father-in-law, with whom, as mentioned above, I had shared my discourse, had kept a copy unbeknownst to me, and since the matter seemed equally delicate and extraordinary to him, he had shared it with this Puki-haï, who passed for the *Socrates* of the Island; and it was in favor of his vast genius that they infringed on the law of not elevating to positions of dignity those who have left the Island. Puki-haï, concerned about the effect that my speech would have over the mind of the masses, which is naturally attracted to novelty, had prepared another one to refute mine. His colleagues couldn't reasonably refuse him a chance to ascend the same tribunal the next day, from which I had preached to the whole population; and he showed the great magnitude of his judgment, and drew on the observations he had made on his travels.

He had all the success he had hoped for: he didn't refute my proofs, but he persuaded his fellow-citizens of the need to live as their fathers had done. Everyone applauded him, and he was given the title of defender of the truth. Which didn't keep me from gaining the esteem of all the Adoë-Rezi, and even of the Puki-haï himself. But, the Supreme Magistrate begged me never to speak again about the God I had proclaimed to them, or his worship, either in public, or in private. I promised this, and I've kept my promise strictly.

But, forever occupied with the desire to procure some advantage for this happy people, I resolved to teach it many useful things they were ignorant of, such as printing, pottery, grafting: but since I didn't know much about these things, I resolved to cross the sea again, to learn these things properly. I shared my intentions with my father-in-law, and with Puki-haï, who had become my close friend. I explained to them the advantages that could be found in these things. I begged them to obtain leave from the Supreme Magistrate to cross the sea again with the next spies sent to Asia; and I took all the most inviolable oaths to return to the rendezvous at the precise time for which it was arranged. They had no trouble obtaining this permission; and I departed Ajao near the end of June 1680. When I arrived in Asia, I could have stopped anywhere in China, India, or even Batavia, but a vestige of love for my homeland drew me onward. I didn't find my compatriots any better than I had left them: on the contrary, they now seemed twice as corrupt to me. This may be because I was now accustomed to the morals of Ajao, and everything else looks like vice to me. However that may be, I have hastened to educate myself those things I had come to seek a personal knowledge of; and I have whiled away my leisure writing this short history to satisfy a friend's curiosity. At present, now that I have a rather complete knowledge of what my fellow-citizens lack, I will depart for Ajao, and I hope to rejoin my fellow-citizens, my wives, my children, and my friends; to go there and change parchment to paper, to print the hymns and odes of the Ajaoians myself; to establish potteries in the quarter of Peridi; and to teach these happy plowmen how to multiply their trees by grafting: aside from the fact that I bring many sorts of seeds they don't know of, and whose fruits are very healthy. Ultimately, I will spend the rest of my days far from superstition, ambition, greed and slander; in a word, among men who may not descend from Adam at all, since they don't feel the force of our insane passions. And, when motion, ceasing in my person, numbers me among the dead, I will cry for joy, at the completion of this tiresome pilgrimage: "*I have been, and I will no longer be.*"

Completed on 4 December 1682.

A FRAGMENT OF WHAT FONTENELLE CALLED HIS "REPUBLIC"

I.[31]

Nobody can attain the public Charges unless they are wealthy to a certain degree; two thousand *écus* in income, for example.

When a Post has been attained, one's wealth will go to those who would inherit it if they were dead, and they will live from a public stipend.

---

[31] Published in *Œuvres de Monsieur de Fontenelle*, Volume 9 (1766); online at:
https://books.google.com/books?id=tfMNAAAAYAAJ

If they have children who are minors, they will be, as for their property, under the guardianship of their nearest relative.

A certain part of the Magistrate's wealth will be inalienable during his life, to preserve it for any children he might have after he takes up his Duties.

II.

A man who offers to cultivate the lands of another, which are better than what he already has, will be accepted there, while paying its Proprietor what income they produce for him. At the end of three years the Proprietor can take them back, if he wants; and if he doesn't take sufficient advantage of them, after three years he can be outbid in this way.

III.

It will only be those whose wealth is above two thousand *écus* in income who will pay certain taxes according to what they own surpassing two thousand *écus*; and these taxes will be the only subsidies of the State.

IV.

The son of a Magistrate can never be one.

V.

There will be no Nobles or Commoners.

All professions will be equally honorable, and Magistrates might equally be taken from theirs, from the moment the prescribed wealth is gained.

VI.

There will only be three orders of Magistrates.

The first and lowest will judge without appeal all the civil trials of Individuals, and will regulate the Police.

The second will judge the Judgments of the first in their trials. Each Judgment given will be printed, along with the Parties' arguments and the detailed arguments of all the Judges. This Judgment will never be overturned; but Judges found to have been of a mistaken view a certain number of times, will be withdrawn. They will never regain their property, but they will receive a small pension from the Public.

These second Magistrates will review all trials with the death penalty, and the judgment of the first won't be confirmed unless they confirm it.

They will be in charge of the public buildings, festivals, shows, etc.

There will only be three of the last kind of Magistrates, and Sovereignty will reside in their persons. They will be called the three Ministers of the State. Things will be passed among them with a plurality of votes. They will be able to depose those of the second order. They will be in charge of peace and war. At the age of seventy they will have no further functions, and will be deposed.

VII.

Each City will have its own Magistrates of the first order; they will be elected with a plurality of votes of all the fathers in the city, not in an assembly, but by ballots taken to all the houses.

When the Magistrate of the second order, or State Councilor is to be elected, the three Ministers will choose him from a number composed of all the four most senior Judges of each City.

And for the election of a Minister, each of the Cities will send a Deputy, and all these Deputies will choose the Minister from the Body of State Councilors.

VIII.

All the Citizens will be soldiers, and under obligation to go to war.

There will be set times for all of them to exercise, to be ready in case of need: in addition, there will always be a standing army, composed of perpetual soldiers.

The three Ministers will hand out all the Duties of the army, according to the soldiers' seniority or fine deeds.

The troops will only be paid by the Treasurers sent by the Ministers.

The Generals will indispensably have risen through all the ranks. They will be perpetual.

Their children will never be able to ascend above the rank of Captain, nor will those of the Ministers.

IX.

A man who has committed a misdeed will be ineligible for all public Posts, and will lose those he already had, unless he finds a way to provide some signal service to the State.

A misdeed means an extraordinary perfidy against someone; breaking one's word on an important matter; denying a deposit, etc.

Even if three affairs happen to him, where, although he can't be convicted, appearances are very strong against him, that will pass for a misdeed.

X.

Statues will be erected to the Great Men, in some form, as well as to beautiful Women. They might even, for the sake of greater resemblance, preserve all their figures in wax in a magnificent Palace made for the purpose.

These Statues or Figures will be tried for things that didn't merit corporeal punishment, and this would constitute a great dishonor.

XI.

Girls will have nothing in marriage.

If a young man performed a fine deed of any kind, he will have a right to select whatever girl he likes in his City; she will not be under any obligation to marry him, but she will not be able to marry anyone else for a year, unless he gives his consent, or another who has performed an even finer deed takes her for himself.

Women will be able to repudiate their husbands, without being able to be repudiated, but they will have to wait a year before they can remarry.

XII.

Often holding spectacles for the People, Opera, Plays, and some even of a new kind, such as representing truly and on the basis of historical documents, a Roman Triumph, a Sacrifice, etc. Also portraying, in a true manner, the most pompous or extraordinary things from Foreign Countries: the Persian's Feast of *Ali*, the Mogol having himself weighed, etc.

Also showing the People the absurdity of all that is opposed to their morals and government.

XIII.

No Orators in the whole State but certain Orators paid by the Public, whose job is to occasionally tell the People of the goodness of their government, explaining the reasons for all its Laws, showing their necessity, offering praise to the Great Men after their death, but all this without getting worked up or the other usual excesses of our Orators.

XIV.

Individuals will plead their cases themselves, or will have them pleaded, but in a very simple manner, by one of their friends.

There will only be a very small number of Laws for the goods which all brothers will share equally, for example, etc. The rest will be judged *ex aequo et bono*.

ANOTHER FRAGMENT

I.

The Magistrate of the first and lowest order will only be unable to acquire any money by refusing their entire annual pension, and giving to the State the rest.

The Magistrate of the second order won't be able to do this. The higher the Magistrate rises in dignity, the more he must diminish in wealth and means of acquisition.

II.

There will be appeals in criminal, but not in civil law. A civil judgment won't be overturned, but the Judges will be punished. If the judgment is declared unjust, the first Judges who were of the wrong opinion, will pay a sum to the complainant party, who will reciprocally pay them that much, if it loses.

At the year's end those judgments will be looked into which have drawn complaints, which Judges have most often had the wrong opinion. Based on how often they have failed in their post, they will be demoted or suspended.

There will be judgments which won't be declared completely unjust, but only blameworthy.

III.

The nominations to a Body, as of the Robe or the Sword, will occur in this Body, up to a certain point beyond which they will pass to another Body, because to that point one might base themselves on reputation; beneath which one cannot. The Men of the Robe will name the high Officers of the Troops. The Troops will name the high Officers of the Robe.

IV.

Bodies of Negotiators. They will be made to travel while young. Then at small Embassies, then larger ones. After which they will be of the Council of foreign affairs. They will lose their property or part of it by entering into the large Embassies.

V.

The Supreme Council of three, Sword, Robe, Negotiators. Immediately beneath, Councils which will examine and digest all sorts of affairs to report them to the Ruler. Finances, War, Marines, foreign affairs, Trade, Arts, Laws.

www.ingramcontent.com/pod-product-compliance
Lightning Source LLC
Chambersburg PA
CBHW031109250726
48655CB00004B/1642